VOICES AGAINST TYRANNY

Writing of the Spanish Civil War

VOICES AGAINST TYRANNY

Writing of the Spanish Civil War

With an Introduction by

STEPHEN SPENDER

Edited by

JOHN MILLER

SCRIBNER **SIGNATURE** EDITION

CHARLES SCRIBNER'S SONS   NEW YORK

1986

Library of Congress Cataloging-in-Publication Data
Voices against tyranny.
   1. Spain—History—Civil War, 1936-1939—Literary
collections.   I. Miller, John.
PN6071.S6V65   1986   808.8'0358   86-6528
ISBN 0-684-18697-7
ISBN 0-684-18698-5 (pbk.)

Published simultaneously in Canada by
Collier Macmillan Canada, Inc.
Composition by Maryland Linotype Composition Co.
  Baltimore, Maryland

Cover painting "Elegy to the Spanish Republic, No. 34,"
1953-4, oil on canvas, 80 × 100", by Robert Motherwell,
Albright Knox Art Gallery, Buffalo, New York. Gift of
Seymour H. Knox, 1957.

Special thanks to Heidi Benson

CONTENTS

CONTENTS

ix

VOICES AGAINST TYRANNY

Writing of the Spanish Civil War

INTRODUCTION

The outbreak of the Spanish Civil War in July 1936, with the attempt by the group of Spanish generals led by General Franco to make a *pronunciamiento* overthrowing the Spanish Republic, resulted almost from the start in introducing onto Spanish soil two separate but coinciding wars. The first of these was purely Spanish, a continuation of the age-old struggle of the great Spanish landowners—aristocrats and leaders of the church hierarchy—with the peasants and (of recent times) the industrial workers. There was also the further complication of the struggle of the Basques and Catalonians for independence from the centralizers of Madrid.

The second war was the projection into Spain, partly as a rehearsal for world war, of the international conflict in Europe between Fascists and anti-Fascists. As the Civil War went on, its international aspects loomed larger, with increasing support of Franco by Nazi Ger-

1

many and increasing interference in the government of the Republic by the Russians.

There was also, on the Republican side, an ideological struggle between Communist Marxists and several varieties of anarchists. Whether they sympathized with Communists or anarchists affected the attitudes of non-Spanish supporters of the Republic. Thus Ernest Hemingway and John Dos Passos quarreled, because Hemingway, though himself no Communist, accepted for strategic reasons the Communist military policy in Spain, (He said, "I like the Communists when they're soldiers, I hate them when they're priests.") Dos Passos bitterly resented the execution by Communist agents of his friend the anarchist leader José Robles, whereas Hemingway accepted it as a necessary consequence of the war of ideologies. Kingsley Martin, editor of the left-wing English periodical *The New Statesman*, refused to print work by George Orwell in which Orwell took the side of the POUM (Partido Obrero de Unificación Marxista [United Marxist Workers Party]), some of whose members had been shot down by the Republican militia in June 1937—a kind of miniature civil war within the Civil War.

There were bitter disagreements among the Republicans in Spain as also among their supporters abroad; there was criminal negligence among those in authority in the Republic (as Arthur Koestler documented in his description of the fall of Malaga) and, worst of all, there were atrocities on the Republican side perhaps equalling those committed by the rebels. (Hugh Thomas, the noted historian of the War, thinks atrocities were as bad on both sides; Antony Beevor thinks that those on Franco's side were worse.) It may seem astonishing, therefore, that long after the war the Republic still appeared, in the minds of those who supported it, the most just and least corrupt cause of the present century.

A somewhat cynical explanation for this might be that Fascism at the time was already known to be so bad (the evils of Stalin did not show themselves fully until later) that the combination of Hitler/Mussolini/Franco had the effect of whitewashing all the deeds of their opponents, however bad. A deeper reason is that the Spanish Civil War, though a great public-political event, was for many Republicans and for most non-Spanish anti-Fascists a very personal involvement. Their reasons for supporting the Republic (to them, simply "Spain") were moral before they were political. Indeed, anti-Fascism filled a kind of moral void of the democracies that had failed to stand up for the basic principles of freedom. The anti-Fascist supporters of Spain were responding to the call of Spanish democracy attacked by totalitarian powers, whereas the leaders of the democracies, of which they were citizens, failed to do so. Worse, the English and French governments, through the activities of the notorious Non-intervention Committee in London, were actually aiding Franco—the English in particular, being obsessed at this time with fear of annoying Hitler. Anticipating the Second World War, they hoped that Hitler's hunger for Lebensraum might still be directed against Russia rather than the West. To them, the salvation of England lay in sitting back and letting the Fascists win.

In the eyes of the anti-Fascists, for England and France to prevent arms from reaching the Republic when Germany and Italy were openly sending not only arms but armies to Franco was worse than hypocrisy—it was betrayal of democracy everywhere, which would, they thought, if the Republicans lost the war, mean the spread of Fascism all over Europe. The knowledge that Russia was sending arms to the Republicans did not alter this anti-Fascist fear, since geographically and economically Russia was in a worse position to help the Republic than were Germany and Italy to help Franco. This was a period when the democracies were doing less than nothing to support democracy, when liberals who tried to remain neutral in the struggle seemed to be equating liberalism with apathy, and when Russia appeared as the sole power against totalitarianism like that triumphant in central Europe.

There is a crucial distinction to be made between the anti-Fascism of 1936–1939 (the duration of the Spanish Civil War) and that after September 1939, following the outbreak of the Second World War. After 1939, anti-Fascism became the official policy of the democracies. In 1936, it was a movement of individuals, organized, it is true, by numerous committees for "Spain" and, beyond them, the "Front Populaire" in Paris. In all these activities the Communists kept well in the background.

Although the Spanish people, in resisting the generals' rising, led by Franco, were supporting their elected government, in doing so, they were also acting as individuals, for they were in the classic situation that may occur in Hispanic countries when a government that is widely held to have failed to maintain public order is overthrown by the army and succeeded by a military dictatorship. This is a *pronunciamiento*. It was as individuals that the Spanish soldiers, sailors, citizens, and peasants in half of Spain refused to surrender to Franco. The exiles from Germany and Italy who went to Spain and formed the Thaelmann and Garibaldi battalions of the International Brigade (organized by the Communist

International in September 1939) were seizing the historic opportunity to fight back as individuals against dictators who had sent their comrades into concentration camps and from whom they themselves had escaped into bitter exile. And it was as individuals who had, by joining the International Brigade, forfeited their every right to protection by the British government that writers and poets like Christopher Caudwell, John Cornford, Ralph Fox, and Julian Bell went to Spain to fight on the Republican side. All died there. The American Communist Party began its organization of what was to become the Abraham Lincoln battalion in November 1936, after the Thaelmann column had already gone into battle. Its first contingent left on the *Normandie* on December 26 and by the first week in January 1937 was parading with other International volunteers down the Ramblas in Barcelona.

So the Spanish Civil War, in both its national and international aspects, had for thousands of people all over the world the appearance of being a direct confrontation between good and evil, right and wrong, freedom and tyranny. Something of this feeling of a crusade brushed off onto the very distinguished group of American reporters of the war who were situated in Madrid: Ernest Hemingway, his wife-to-be Martha Gellhorn, Lillian Hellman, and Josephine Herbst. "Spain" certainly brought out in Hemingway not only his courage but his great imagination and powerful intelligence. It must be admitted, too, that the Falangist supporters of Franco, basking in the blessings bestowed on them by the church, also saw it as a holy war and were supported in this by their few foreign sympathizers and volunteers. The philosopher George Santayana wrote, answering a correspondent:

Spain has always been the most unfortunate of countries, and it is now having a hard struggle to throw the Bolshies off, that had got hold of her always execrable government. But my friends write that the young people are unrecognizable in their energy and discipline and that we shall soon see a new Spain as vigorous as in the Middle Ages. And of course Spain would not be alone in the transformation.

—From a letter written from Mussolini's Rome, 1936; presumably not written as a joke.

Such medievalist black fervor can be set against Thomas Mann's introduction to an anthology called "Spain" published by the Socialist Alliance of Swiss Women:

I shall be asked what I mean by "spirit" and what by "interest." Well, then: the spiritual, seen from the politico-social angle is the longing of the people for better, juster, happier conditions of life, more adequate to the developed human consciousness. It is this longing, affirmed by all those who are of good will. And "interest" is all that seeks to thwart this consummation, because it would thereby be cut off from certain advantages and privileges, seeks by every means at its command, not scorning the basest, even the criminal, or, well knowing that in the end it must fail, tries to put off as long as it can the evil day—for a little while, for a few decades. In Spain interest rages. Rages with a shamelessness such as the world has seldom seen. What has been happening there for many months is one of the most scandalous and mortifying pages which history has to show. Does the world see it, feel it? Only very partially.

Here, writing from Switzerland, Thomas Mann is seeing the Spanish Civil War as a microcosm of a Manichaean conflict between the forces of good and evil in the contemporary world—a view to which the character of Hitler surely lent force. Spain, that sunburned landscape cut off from the rest of Europe, historic home of saints, fanatics, and decadent monarchs, stimulated the imagination of the world. The idea of Apocalypse haunts the pages of André Malraux's novel about Spain, *L'Espoir* (translated under the title *Man's Hope*), as it does the pages of the Civil War in Gustav Regler's memorable autobiography *The Owl of Minerva*.

For those non-Spaniards who went to Spain during the Civil War, the spectacle of the Spanish people was deeply moving. Most of these non-Spaniards were on the Republican side, though Roy Campbell's account of the liberation of Toledo from the Reds (and the horrors of the Red occupation before this) suggests that either side could strike the foreigner as heroic. Campbell's account of this episode strikes me as having an authenticity not present when he is evoking scenes of his own heroism.

W. H. Auden's description of Valencia (*The New Statesman*, January 30, 1937) could be multiplied by similar descriptions of Barcelona written by George Orwell, Cyril Connolly, and myself. We all discovered in ourselves feelings best expressed by Wordsworth in "The Prelude," describing his reaction to scenes he witnessed in France in the early days of the Revolution: "Bliss was it in that dawn to be alive."

Auden sums up his impressions of Valencia in words that I would have found equally applicable to Barcelona.

In the last six months these people have been learning what it is to inherit their own country, and once a man has tasted freedom he will not lightly give it up: freedom to choose for himself and organize his life. . . . That is why, only eight hours away at the gates of Madrid where this wish to live has no possible expression than the will to kill, General Franco has already lost two professional armies and is in the process of losing a third.

Auden was to tell Monroe Spears some years later, when Spears was writing a book about him, that when he was in Spain, he was far more shaken than he had ever realized he was capable of being by the sight of churches that had been destroyed by the Republicans. The full realization of the shock was probably a delayed reaction. Looking back on Spanish events now, I feel that although there was something authentic about our Wordsworthian recognition of the joy of the people's freedom achieved, that we could not see any of the terrible murders happening behind this scene of revolution reinforces one of the great lessons of this century: that there is no trust to be placed in travellers' impressions of popular rejoicing soon after revolution.

Probably, too, if we had seen Valencia or Barcelona in the fall of 1936 and not in the spring of 1937, we would have had a less happy impression, for what we saw would have been chaos. Luis Buñuel, seeing the first days of the revolution, which, as he writes, "I personally had so ardently desired," relates that all he felt was shock:

Elie Faure, the famous art historian and an ardent supporter of the Republican cause, came to Madrid for a few days. I went to visit him one morning at his hotel and can still see him standing at his window in his long underwear, watching the demonstrations in the street below and weeping at the sight of the people in arms. One day, we watched a hundred peasants marching by, four abreast, some armed with hunting rifles and revolvers, some with sickles and pitchforks. In an obvious effort at discipline, they were trying very hard to march in step. It seemed as if nothing could defeat such a deep-seated popular force, but the joy and enthusiasm that colored those early days soon gave way to arguments, disorganization and uncertainty—all of which lasted until November 1936, when an efficient and disciplined Republican organization began to emerge.

There may have been some efficiency after November 1936 in Madrid and some show of it in Valencia. But where else? Certainly not in Malaga before its fall to the Nationalists, as Arthur Koestler describes it in his terrifying account of the capture of that city by the Nationalists, still the most moving of all the documents bearing witness to the agony that was "Spain." Hemingway's *For Whom the Bell Tolls* does not approach it as felt truth, although Hemingway made a heroic effort to give a detached, complex, and objective picture of the war. It seems to me, however, that his novel, though magnificent, sinks under the weight of the effort. The point of view being Hemingway's own, he must need have an American hero, Robert Jordan, who embodies Hemingway's own qualities—Robert Jordan is a strategist, a great lover, has shrewd political insight, is a writer, and while supporting the Republic, is also a Catholic. Moreover, much of the Spanish dialogue in the novel between Jordan and the Spanish characters is rendered into an English that reads like a literal translation of a Spanish grammar made by a Spaniard who does not know English.

Much of the literature of the Spanish Civil War written on the Republican side seems to show that the writers of it felt that there was a "truth" of "Spain" that remained independent of, and survived the mold of, Communism into which successive Republican governments were forced. Anti-Fascists who went to Spain and accepted Communism there as inevitable on the grounds of political exigence—and who later changed their minds about this, becoming anti-Communists—nevertheless retained their belief in the justice of the Republican cause. They did not renounce "Spain." This is true even of Arthur Koestler, who certainly experienced the worst that both sides had to offer. He became virulently anti-Communist, but he did not regret having supported the Spanish Republic.

The same was true of William Herrick, a veteran of the Lincoln battalion who was severely wounded outside Madrid, whose novel *Hermanos!* is both bitterly anti-Communist and profoundly sympathetic to the Spanish Republic. On the other hand, another veteran of the Lincoln battalion (and later one of the Hollywood Ten), the late Alvah Bessie, who wrote an affecting memoir of the war, *Men in Battle*, remained sympathetic to his old comrades.

Auden was one of those who, during the weeks that he was in Spain, seems to have accepted Communist policy as inevitable and necessary. This is what his poem "Spain" is surely about. In it he interprets the Civil War along strictly Marxist lines, seeing in it the classic "revolutionary situation." His reading of the war is in terms of historical materialism: Thesis (medieval Spain and the European past) = yesterday, that is, Franco. Antithesis (the struggle going on today against these obscurantist forces) = the Spanish Republic: "Today the struggle." Synthesis = tomorrow, when the Republic has won, through Communism, and after the Revolution (whose means have to be accepted as necessary), there is the withering away of the political state and entry into the post-political world of happy and virtuous Anarchy: "The walks by the lake, the weeks of perfect communion."

Auden combines in this poem the logic of Marxist theory with his own poetic logic of imagery evocative of past, present, future, concentrating on "Spain" in 1937—"Today the struggle." But in doing so, he arrives, quite logically, at conclusions that, politically "correct," are alien to the poetic imagination, perhaps even alien to humanity, to what George Orwell called "decency." Accepting the Marxist view that Freedom is the recognition of Necessity, he grimly faces Necessity:

> Today the deliberate increase in the
> chances of death.
> The conscious acceptance of guilt in the
> necessary murder.

Orwell seized on these lines to attack Auden for being an intellectual who approved of murder. By murder Orwell was here thinking of—or chose to pretend he was thinking of—the kind of murders then occurring in Spain as acts of private terrorism: someone being taken for a ride in a car into the country near Barcelona at night, then shot to death and his body thrown into a ditch. (Cyril Connolly told me that he knew a rather mysterious Englishman, come to Barcelona as an anarchist sympathizer, who told him that being suspected by his comrades of espionage, he was taken as passenger on a car ride of this kind every night to see some suspect murdered—as a warning to him.)

Auden could reasonably point out that when he wrote of "accepting" the "necessary murder," he did not mean terrorist acts of killing, merely that if you support revolution, you support murder. If you object to murder in war or revolution, you are a pacifist, and in "Spain" he has to recognize that he is not pacifist. Moreover, he might have argued, "Spain" is a poem about Historic Necessity, and the word "necessary" in such a context is almost inseparable from the word "murder." But surely he came to agree with Orwell to the extent of feeling that his conscientious attempt to politicize his poetry in support of "Spain" had led him into very alien territory. The fusion of political with poetic logic led out of poetry into the politics of exigence. He defended himself (rather unhappily) from Orwell's charges, but he brought against himself a (to him) still graver charge—of using poetry to tell lies. "Spain" ended with the lines:

> *History to the defeated*
> *May say alas but cannot help or pardon.*

Many years later, seeing a copy of the original pamphlet of his poem "Spain" (sold for Spanish relief) on a friend's bookshelf, he took it down and wrote, "This is a lie," against the last two lines. Poetry is, or can be, of course, history; but in poetry the defeated are not made non-persons, as they well may be in politics and as they are in Orwell's *1984*. In poetry, on the contrary, the defeated are often celebrated, given immortality.

After "Spain," Auden abandoned the attempt to fuse poetry with politics.

The English poets who joined the International Brigade considered that the necessity of fighting Fascism had become a more urgent task for them than writing poetry. If they continued to write it, they justified themselves for doing so by putting their poetry at the service of their politics. Many died too young for their views about politics and the war to develop beyond their initial sense of dedication to the cause, or even to see far beyond the international struggle against German, Italian, and Spanish Fascism to the particular Spanish tragedy (that which Hemingway made his tragic attempt to grasp in *For Whom the Bell Tolls*). John Cornford, however, wrote a kind of political poetry that, if he had lived, might have brought something new to modern poetry—the poetry of the intellectual will of the poet immersed in the class struggle. His poems were partly those of a soldier dedicated to the cause for which he was fighting and trying to steel his will by constantly reminding himself of the Fascist enemy. On the evening of battle, he prays (prays to what? To the party? To Karl Marx? All one can say is, he prays):

> *Though Communism was my waking time,*
> *Always before the lights of home*
> *Shone clear and steady and full in view*
> *Here, if you fall, there's help for you—*
> *Now, with my Party, I stand alone.*
>
> *Then let my private battle with my nerves*
> *The fear of pain whose pain survives,*
> *The love that tears me by the roots,*
> *The loneliness that claws my guts,*
> *Fuse in the welded front our sight preserves.*

In other poems he tries to enter into the objective development of history, his own personality becoming, as it were, absorbed into it. This points to a kind of metaphysical secular poetry, materialist, yet in a humanist or Communist way, religious.

Of all the tragedies of the war perhaps the greatest was that of the destruction of what was surely a twentieth-century Renaissance of all the arts in Spain, particularly poetry. García Lorca, killed in the first few months of the war, is the outstanding figure in this Renaissance. As a result of his having been murdered in Granada, to which he had fled, his name has been used as a symbol of anti-Fascist martyrdom. But his death was perhaps the result of the terrible confusion of the early part of the war in which the highly politicized atmosphere of the time—on all sides—made it possible for random murders to appear to be the results of responsible political decisions. When I was in Republican Spain in 1937, I noticed that most of the poets whom I met there, while they talked endlessly of Lorca, whom they all loved and who was the subject of innumerable witty anecdotes, avoided drawing any political moral from his murder, as though they considered it obscene to use his death as political propaganda against Fascism.

Although, through his work in the theater—taking his plays to villages for performance to the workers—Lorca was a popular, almost a populist, writer; he was not a political figure. His great poem, "Death of a Bullfighter," written before the Civil War, can, in its somber evocation of a tragic Spain, be taken almost as a prelude to the drama of the war, taking death and violence, in the context of the bullfight, as its themes. It has a greatness similar to Picasso's painting *Guernica*. But having written this prelude so prophetic of the tragedy to come, Lorca, the poet who enchanted his fellow poets, not merely this side of idolatry but still more remarkably beyond literary jealousy, disappears from the scene, like Harlequin in the theater, through a trap door, or like Shakespeare's Ariel.

When I was attending the Congress of Intellectuals at Madrid in 1937, I happened to find on a bookstall an early volume of poems by Rafael Alberti. It was called, if I remember rightly, *Sobre los Angelos*. I took it to him to inscribe for me. As he did so, he said, sighing, "Ah, I was a poet then," by which I took him to mean that while dedicating all his poetic gifts to the winning of the war (he was a fervent Communist), he had a sense of poetic loss.

A great deal of propagandist literature was written by Spanish poets during the Civil War. But it always seemed to me that the best Spanish poets (one being my friend Manual Altolaguirre) shrank from the extremes of anti-Fascist politicization of literature that the non-Spanish internationalist supporters of Spain imposed on it. The Spaniards did not write the kind of Communist anti-Fascist poetry fixing on Spain as its subject that was written then by French Communist poets—such as Aragon and Paul Eluard.

What the Spanish poets had to do was not be ideologists of propaganda but to burn in the flame of Spain's martyrdom, producing from it a cry beyond politics. There was one poet who did this—Miguel Hernández, a soldier fighting on the Madrid front. His is the authentic voice of "Spain" beyond ideology, where everything is reduced to the humanity acting and acted upon, pure witnessing of the most terrible events, the most outrageous injustices inflicted. In this poetry the war that was "Spain" becomes one with the international anti-

Fascist war, because international anti-Fascism is seen as the response of the nations beyond Spain to the martyred Republic.

> *Nations of the earth, fatherlands of the sea, brothers*
> *Of the world, and of nothing:*
> *inhabitants lost and more distant*
> *From the sight than from the heart.*
>
> *Here I have a voice impassioned*
> *Here I have a life, challenged and indignant,*
> *Here I have a message, here I have a life.*

This is poetry hammered out of suffering, whose truth seems beyond dispute, outside politics, like certain poems of Whitman in *Drum Taps*. No wonder that Hernández died in prison where he was confined for years after the end of the war. "Spain" survives in his poetry.

Most of the writers of the Spanish twentieth-century Renaissance were scattered throughout the world after the war. They went into exile in France, in Latin and North America, in Russia. The line of this great intellectual flowering was broken. One consolation may perhaps be found, though, in the fact that the Spanish Civil War awoke among the writers of Latin America a consciousness of Spanish as a world literature which, during those years, became centered on the Spanish Republic in the writing of Pablo Neruda, Octavio Paz, and others. Perhaps "Spain" reborn into the world of the once worldwide Spanish Empire will enjoy another Renaissance in the world literature of the twenty-first century.

—Stephen Spender

W. H. AUDEN

Impressions of Valencia

The pigeons fly about the square in brilliant sunshine, warm as a fine English May. In the centre of the square, surrounded all day long by crowds and surmounted by a rifle and fixed bayonet, fifteen feet high is an enormous map of the Civil War, rather prettily illustrated after the manner of railway posters urging one to visit Lovely Lakeland or Sunny Devon. Badajoz is depicted by a firing-party; a hanged man represents Huelva; a doll's train and lorry are heading for Madrid; at Seville Quiepo el [*sic*] Llano is frozen in an eternal broadcast. The General seems to be the Little Willie of the war; in a neighbouring shop window a strip of comic wood-cuts shows his rake's progress from a perverse childhood to a miserable and well-merited end.

Altogether it is a great time for the poster artist and there are some very good ones. Cramped in a little grey boat the Burgos Junta, dapper Franco and his bald German adviser, a cardinal and two ferocious Moors are busy hanging Spain; a green Fascist centipede is caught in the fanged trap of Madrid; in photomontage a bombed baby lies couchant upon a field of aeroplanes.

Today a paragraph in the daily papers announces that since there have been incidents at the entrances to cabarets, these will in future be closed at 9 p.m. Long streamers on the public buildings appeal for unity, determination, and discipline. Three children, with large brown eyes like some kind of very rich sweet, are playing trains round the fountain. On one of the Ministries a huge black arrow draws attention to the fact that the front at Teruel is only 150 kilometres away. This is the Spain for which charming young English aviators have assured us that the best would be a military dictatorship backed by a foreign Power.

Since the Government moved here the hotels are crammed to bursting with officials, soldiers, and journalists. There are porters at the station and a few horsecabs, but no taxis, in order to save petrol. Food is plentiful, indeed an hotel lunch is heavier than one could wish. There is a bullfight in aid of the hospitals; there is a variety show where an emaciated-looking tap-dancer does an extremely sinister dance of the machine guns. The foreign correspondents come in for their dinner, conspicuous as actresses.

And everywhere there are people. They are here in corduroy breeches with pistols on their hip, in uniform, in civilian suits and berets. They are here, sleeping in the hotels, eating in the restaurants, in the cafés drinking and having their shoes cleaned. They are here, driving fast cars on business, running the trains and the trams, keeping the streets clean, doing all those things that the gentry cannot believe will be properly done unless they are there to keep an eye on them. This is the bloodthirsty and unshaven Anarchy of the bourgeois cartoon, the end of civilization from which Hitler has sworn to deliver Europe.

For a revolution is really taking place, not an odd shuffle or two in cabinet appointments. In the last six months these people have been learning what it is to inherit their own country, and once a man has tasted freedom he will not lightly give it up; freedom to choose for himself and to organize his life, freedom not to depend for good fortune on a clever and outrageous piece of overcharging or a windfall of drunken charity. That is why, only eight hours away at the gates of Madrid where this wish to live has no possible alternative expression than the power to kill, General Franco has already lost two professional armies and is in the process of losing a third.

While serving as a stretcher-bearer for the Republicans, W. H. Auden wrote "Impressions of Valencia" for The New Statesman and Nation *(January 1937) as well as the controversial poem "Spain" (April 1937), which appears here on page 211. In his later years, Auden regretted the political rhetoric of the poem and would not allow it to be reprinted. Only after his death did it reappear.*

JOHN DOS PASSOS

Room and Bath at the Hotel Florida

I wake up suddenly with my throat stiff. It's not quite day. I am lying in a comfortable bed, in a clean well-arranged hotel room staring at the light indigo oblong of the window opposite. I sit up in bed. Again there's the hasty loudening shriek, the cracking roar, the rattle of tiles and a tinkling shatter of glass and granite fragments. Must have been near because the hotel shook. My room is seven or eight stories up. The hotel is on a hill. From the window I can look out at all the old part of Madrid over the crowded tiled roofs, soot-color flecked with pale yellow and red under the metal blue before dawn gloaming. The packed city stretches out sharp and still as far as I can see, narrow roofs, smokeless chimney-pots, buffcolored towers with cupolas and the pointed slate spires of seventeencentury Castile. Everything is cut out of metal in the steely brightening light. Again the shriek, the roar, rattle, tinkle of a shell bursting somewhere. Then silence again, cut only by the thin yelps of a hurt dog, and very slowly from one of the roofs below a smudge of dirty yellow smoke forms, rises, thickens and spreads out in the still air under the low indigo sky. The yelping goes weakly on and on.

It's too early to get up. I try going to bed again, fall asleep to wake almost immediately with the same tight throat, the same heavy feeling in my chest. The shells keep coming in. They are small but they are damn close. Better get dressed. The water's running in the bathroom, though the hot's not on yet. A man feels safe shaving, sniffing the little customary odor of the usual shaving soap in the clean bathroom. After a bath and a shave I put on my bathrobe, thinking after all this is what the Madrileños have been having instead of an alarmclock for five months now, and walk downstairs to see what the boys are up to. The shells keep coming in. The hotel, usually so quiet at this time, is full of scamper and confusion.

Everywhere doors fly open onto the balconies round the central glassed over well. Men and women in various stages of undress are scuttling out of front rooms, dragging suitcases and mattresses into back rooms. There's a curlyhaired waiter from the restaurant who comes out of several different doors in succession each time with his arm round a different giggling or sniveling young woman. Great exhibitions of dishevelment and lingerie.

Downstairs the correspondents are stirring about sleepily. An Englishman is making coffee on an electric coffeepot that speedily blows out the fuse at the same time melting the plug. A Frenchman in pajamas is distributing grapefruit to all and sundry from the door of his room.

The shells keep coming in. Nobody seems to know how to get at the coffee until a completely dressed woman novelist from Iowa takes charge of it and distributes it around in glasses with some scorched toast and halves of the Frenchman's grapefruit. Everybody gets lively and talkative until there's no more coffee left. By that time the shelling has died down a little and I go back to bed to sleep for an hour.

When I woke up again everything was quiet. There was hot water in the bathroom. From somewhere among the closepacked roofs under the window there drifted up a faint taste of sizzling olive oil. Round the balconies in the hotel everything was quiet and normal. The pleasantfaced middleaged chambermaids were there in their neat aprons, quietly cleaning. On the lower floor the waiters were serving the morning coffee. Outside on the Plaza de Callao there were some new dents in the pavement that hadn't been there the night before. Somebody said an old newsvendor at the corner had been killed. Yesterday the doorman at the hotel got a spent machinegun bullet in the thigh.

The midmorning sunlight was hot on the Gran Via in spite of the frigid dry wind of Castilian springtime. Stepping out of doors into the bustling jangle of the city I couldn't help thinking of other Madrids I'd known, twenty years ago, eighteen years ago, four years ago. The streetcars are the same, the longnose sallow Madrileño faces are the same, with the same mixture of brown bulletheaded countrymen, the women in the dark-colored shawls don't look very different. Of course you don't see the Best People any more. They are in Portugal and Seville or in their graves. Never did see many this early anyway. The shellholes and the scars made by flying fragments and shrapnel have not changed the general look of the street, nor have the political posters pasted up on every bare piece of wall, or the fact that people are so scrappily dressed and that there's a predominance of uniforms in khaki and blue denim. It's the usualness of it that gives it this feeling of nightmare. I happen to look up at the hotel my wife and I stayed in the last time we were here. The entrance on the street looks normal and so does the departmentstore next door, but the upper stories of the building, and the story where our room was, are shot as full of holes as a Swiss cheese.

Nobody hurries so fast along the street, and hardly anybody passes along the Gran Via these days without speeding his pace a little because it's the street where most shells fall, without pausing to glance up at the tall NewYorkish telephone building to look for new shellholes. It's funny how the least Spanish building in Madrid, the baroque tower of Wall Street's International Tel and Tel, the symbol of the colonizing power of the dollar, has become in the minds of the Madrileños the symbol of the defense of the city. Five months of intermittent shellfire have done remarkably little damage. There are a few holes and dents but nothing that couldn't be repaired in two weeks. On the side the shelling comes from the windows of several stories have been bricked up. The pompous period ornamentation has hardly been chipped.

Inside you feel remarkably safe. The whole apparatus of the telephone service still goes on in the darkened offices. The elevators run. There's a feeling like Sunday in a New York downtown building. In their big quiet office you find the press censors, a cadaverous Spaniard and a plump little pleasant voiced Austrian woman. They say they are going to move their office to another building. It's too much to ask the newspapermen on the regular services to duck through a barrage every time they have to file a story, and the censors are beginning to feel that Franco's gunners are out after them personally. Only yesterday the Austrian woman came back to find that a shellfragment had set her room on fire and burned up all her shoes, and the censor had seen a woman made mincemeat of beside him when he stepped out to get a bite of lunch. It's not surprising that the censor is a nervous man; he looks underslept and underfed. He talks as if he understood, without taking too much personal pleasure in it, the importance of his position of guardian of those telephones that are the link with happier countries where the civil war is still being carried on by means of gold credits on bankledgers and munitions contracts and conversations on red plush sofas in diplomatic anterooms instead of with six-inch shells and firing squads. He doesn't give the impression of being complacent about his job. But it's hard for one who is more or less of a free agent from a country at peace to talk about many things with men who are chained to the galley benches of a war.

It's a relief to get away from the switchboards of power and walk out in the sunny streets again. If you follow the Gran Via beyond the Plaza de Callao down the hill towards the North station, stopping for a second in an excellent bookshop that's still open for business, you run into your first defense barricade. It is solidly built of cemented pavingstones laid in regular courses high as your head. That's where men will make a last stand and die if the fascists break through.

I walk on down the street. This used to be the pleasantest and quickest way to walk out into the country, down into the shady avenue along the Manzanares where the little fat church stands that has Goya's frescoes in it, and out through the iron gate into the old royal domain of El Pardo. Now it's the quickest way to the front.

At the next barricade there's a small beadyeyed sentry who smilingly asks to see my pass. He's a Cuban. As Americans we talk. Somehow there's a bond between us as coming from the western world.

There are trenches made with sandbags in the big recently finished Plaza de España. The huge straggling bronze statues of Don Quixote and Sancho Panza look out oddly towards the enemy position in Carabanchel. At a barracks building on the corner a bunch from the International Brigade is waiting for chow. French faces, Belgian faces, North of Italy faces; German exiles, bearded men blackened with the sun, young boys; a feeling of energy and desperation comes from them. The dictators have stolen their world from them; they have lost their homes, their families, their hopes of a living or a career; they are fighting back.

Up another little hill is the burned shell of the Montaña Barracks where the people of Madrid crushed the military revolt last July. Then we're looking down the broad rimedge street of the Paseo de Rosales. It used to be one of the pleasantest places in Madrid to live because the four and fivestory apartmenthouses overlooked the valley of the Manzanares and the green trees of the old royal parks and domains. Now it's no man's land. The lines cross the valley below, but if you step out on the Paseo you're in the full view of the enemy on the hills opposite, and the Moors are uncommonly good riflemen.

With considerable speed the sightseers scuttled into a house on the corner. There's the narrow hall and the row of bells and the rather grimy dark stairs of the regular Madrid apartmenthouse, but instead of the apartment of Señor Fulano de Tal on the third floor you open a ground glass door and find . . . the front. The rest of the house has been blown away. The ground glass door opens on air, at your feet a well opens full of broken masonry and smashed furniture, then the empty avenue and beyond across the Manzanares, a magnificent view of the enemy. On the top floor there's a room on that side still intact; looking carefully through the half-shattered shutters we can make out trenches and outposts at the top of the hill, a new government trench halfway up the hill and closing the picture, as always, the great snowy cloudtopped barrier of the Guadarrama. The lines are quiet; not a sound. Through the glasses we can see some militiamen strolling around behind a clump of trees. After all it's lunchtime. They can't be expected to start a battle for the benefit of a couple of sightseers.

Walking back to the hotel through the empty streets of the wrecked quarter back of the Paseo we get a chance to see all the quaint possibilities of shellfire and air-bombing among dwelling houses. The dollshouse effect is the commonest, the front or a side of a house sliced off and touchingly revealing parlors, bedrooms, kitchens, dining rooms, twisted iron beds dangling, elaborate chandeliers hanging over void, a piano suspended in the air, a sideboard with dishes still on it, a mirror with a gilt stucco frame glittering high up in a mass of wreckage where everything else has been obliterated.

After lunch I walk out into the northern part of the city to see the mother of an old friend of mine. It's the same apartment where I have been to visit them in various past trips. The same old maid in black with a starched apron opens the door into the dim white rooms

with the old oak and walnut furniture that remind me
a little of Philip II's rooms in the Escorial. My friend's
mother is much older than when I saw her last, but her
eyes under the handsomely arched still dark eyebrows
are as fine as ever, they have the same black flash when
she talks. With her is an older sister from Andalusia, a
very old whitehaired woman, old beyond conversation.
They have been in Madrid ever since the movement, as
they call it, started. Her son has tried to get her to go
to Valencia where he has duties but she doesn't like to
leave her apartment and she wouldn't like the fascists
to think they'd scared her into running away. Of course
getting food is a nuisance but they are old now and
don't need much, she says. She could even invite me to
lunch if I'd come someday and wouldn't expect to get
too much to eat. She tells me which of the newspapers
she likes; then we fall to talking about the old days
when they lived at El Pardo and her husband the doctor
was alive and I used to walk out to see them through
the beautiful park of liveoaks that always made me feel
as if I were walking through the backgrounds of Velas-
quez's paintings. The park was a royal hunting preserve
and was protected, in those days of the Bourbons, by
mantraps and royal game keepers in Goya costumes.
The deer were tame. Over the tea and the almond paste
cakes we talked of walks in the sierra and skiing and
visits to forgotten dried-up Castilian villages and the
pleasure of looking at the construction of old buildings
and pictures and the poems of Antonio Machado.

As I stepped out into the empty street I heard shelling in the distance again. As a precaution I walked over
to the metrostation and took the crowded train down to
the Gran Via. When I got out of the elevator at the
station I found that there weren't so many people as

usual walking down towards the Calle de Alcalá. There was a tendency to stand in doorways.

I was thinking how intact this part of the town was when, opposite Molinero's, the pastry shop where we used to go in the intermissions of the symphony concerts at the Price Circus and stuff with almond paste and eggyolk and whipped cream pastry in the old days, I found myself stepping off the curb into a pool of blood. Water had been sloshed over it but it remained in red puddles among the cobbles. So much blood must have come from a mule, or several people hit at one time. I walked round it. But what everybody was looking at was the division El Campesino in new khaki uniforms parading up the Calle de Alcalá with flags and Italian guns and trucks captured at Brihuega. The bugles blew and the drums rattled and the flags rippled in the afternoon sunlight and the young men and boys in khaki looked healthy and confident walking by tanned from life at the front and with color stung into their faces by the lashing wind off the sierras. I followed them into the Puerta del Sol that, in spite of the two blocks gutted by incendiary bombs, looked remarkably normal in the late afternoon bustle, full of shoeshine boys and newsvendors and people selling shoelaces and briquets and paper covered books.

On the island in the middle where the metrostation is, an elderly man shined my shoes.

A couple of shells came in behind me far up a street. The dry whacking shocks were followed by yellow smoke and the smell of granite dust that drifted slowly past in the wind. There were no more. Groups of men chatting on the corners went on chatting. Perhaps a few more people decided to take the metro instead of the streetcar. An ambulance passed. The old man went on meticulously shining my shoes.

I began to feel that General Franco's gunner, smoking a cigarette as he looked at the silhouette of the city from the hill at Carabanchel, was taking aim at me personally. At last the old man was satisfied with his work, and set down on his box again to wait for another customer while I walked across the halfmoonshaped square through the thinning crowd, to the old Café de Lisboa. Going in through the engraved glass swinging doors and sitting down on the faded chartreusecolored plush and settling down to read the papers over a glass of vermouth was stepping back twenty-one years to the winter when I used to come out from my cold room at the top of a house on the other corner of the Puerta del Sol and warm up with coffee there during the morning. The papers, naturally, were full of victories; this is wartime. When I come out of the café at seven o'clock closing, and head for the Hotel Florida it's already almost dark. For some reason the city seems safer at night.

The correspondents take their meals in the basement of the Hotel Gran Via almost opposite the Telephone Building. You go in through the unlit lobby and through a sort of pantry and down some back stairs past the kitchen into a cavelike place that still has pink lights and an air of night club jippery about it. There at a long table sit the professional foreign correspondents and the young worldsaviours and the members of foreign radical delegations. At the small tables in the alcoves there tend to be militiamen and internationals on sprees and a sprinkling of young ladies of the between the sheets brigade.

This particular night there's a group of British parlia-

mentary bigwigs, including a duchess at a special table. It's been a big day for them, because General Franco's gunners have bagged more civilians than usual. Right outside of the hotel, in fact under the eyes of the duchess, two peaceful Madrileños were reduced to a sudden bloody mess. A splatter of brains had to be wiped off the glassless revolving doors of the hotel. But stuffed with horrors as they were, the British bigwigs had eaten supper.

In fact they'd eaten up everything there was, so that when the American correspondents began to trickle in with nothing in their stomachs but whiskey and were fed each a sliver of rancid ham, there was a sudden explosion of the spirit of Seventy-six. Why should a goddam lousy etcetera duchess eat three courses when a hardworking American newspaperman has to go hungry.

A slightly punchdrunk little ex-bantamweight prizefighter who was often in the joint wearing a snappy militiaman's uniform, and who had tended in the past to be chummy with the members of the gringo contingent who were generous with their liquor, became our champion and muttered dark threats about closing the place up and having the cooks and waiters sent to the front, lousy profiteers hiding under the skirts of the C.N.T. who were all sons of loose women and saboteurs of the war and worse than fascists, mierda. In the end the management produced a couple of longdead whitings and a plate of spinach which they'd probably been planning to eat themselves, and the fires of revolt died down.

Still in Madrid the easiest thing to get, though it's high in price, is whiskey; so it's on that great national fooddrink that the boys at the other end of the wires tend to subsist. One of the boys who'd been there longest leaned across the table and said plaintively, "Now you won't go home and write about the drunken correspondents, will you?"

Outside the black stone city was grimly flooded with moonlight that cut each street into two oblique sections. Down the Gran Via I could see the flashlight of a patrol and hear them demanding in low voices the password for the night of whoever they met on the sidewalk.

From the west came a scattered hollow popping, soft perforations of the distant horizon. Somewhere not very far away men with every nerve tense were crawling along the dark sides of walls, keeping their heads down in trenches, yanking their right arms back to sling a hand grenade at some creeping shadow opposite. And in all the black houses the children we'd seen playing in the streets were asleep, and the grownups were lying there thinking of lost friends and family and ruins and people they'd loved and of hating the enemy and of hunger and how to get a little more food tomorrow, feeling in the numbness of their blood, in spite of whatever scorn in the face of death, the low unending smoulder of apprehension of a city under siege. And I couldn't help feeling a certain awe, as I took off my clothes in my quiet clean room with electric light and running water and a bathtub, in the face of all these people in this city. I lay down on the bed to read a book but instead stared at the ceiling and thought of the pleasantfaced middleaged chambermaid who'd cleaned my room that morning and made the bed and put everything in order and who'd been coming regularly every day, doing the job ever since the siege began just as she'd done it in the days of Don Alfonso, and wondered where she slept and what about her family and her kids and her man, and how perhaps tomorrow coming to work there'd be that hasty loudening shriek and the street full of dust and splintered stone and instead of coming to work the woman would be just a mashed-out mess of blood and guts to be scooped into a new pine coffin and hurried away. And they'd slosh some water over the cobbles and the death of Madrid would go on. A city under siege is not a very good place for a sightseer. It's a city without sleep.

John Dos Passos was in Madrid during the war, writing and working on the film The Spanish Earth *with Ernest Hemingway and Archibald MacLeish. This article was filed for* Esquire *in January 1938.*

LOUIS MacNEICE

Canto VI

The poem is set in the spring of 1936, the eve of war.

And I Remember Spain
   At Easter ripe as an egg for revolt and ruin
Though for a tripper the rain
   Was worse than the surly or the worried or the
      haunted faces
With writings on the walls—
   Hammer and sickle, Boicot, Viva, Muerra;
With café au lait brimming the waterfalls,
   With sherry, shellfish, omelettes.
With fretted stone the Moor
   Had chiselled for effects of sun and shadow;
With shadows of the poor,
   The begging cripples and the children begging.
The churches full of saints
   Tortured on racks of marble—
The old complaints
   Covered with gilt and dimly lit with candles.

With powerful or banal
  Monuments of riches or repression
And the Escorial
  Cold for ever within like the heart of Philip.
With ranks of dominoes
  Deployed on café tables the whole of Sunday
With cabarets that call the tourist, shows
  Of thighs and eyes and nipples.
With slovenly soldiers, nuns,
  And peeling posters from the last elections
Promising bread or guns
  Or an amnesty or another
Order or else the old
  Glory veneered and varnished
As if veneer could hold
  The rotten guts and crumbled bones together.
And a vulture hung in air
  Below the cliffs of Ronda and below him
His hook-winged shadow wavered like despair
  Across the chequered vineyards.
And the boot-blacks in Madrid
  Kept us half an hour with polish and pincers
And all we did
  In that city was drink and think and loiter.
And in the Prado half-
  wit princes looked from the canvas they had paid for
(Goya had the laugh—
  But can what is corrupt be cured by laughter?)
And the day at Aranjuez
  When the sun came out for once on the yellow river
With Valdepenas burdening the breath
  We slept a royal sleep in the royal gardens;
And at Toledo walked
  Around the ramparts where they throw the garbage

And glibly talked
 Of how the Spaniards lack all sense of business.
And Avila was cold
 And Segovia was picturesque and smelly
And a goat on the road seemed old
 As the rocks or the Roman arches.
And Easter was wet and full
 In Seville and in the ring on Easter Sunday
A clumsy bull and then a clumsy bull
 Nodding his banderillas died of boredom.
And the standard of living was low
 But that, we thought to ourselves, was not our
  business;
All that the tripper wants is the *status quo*
 Cut and dried for trippers.
And we thought the papers a lark
 With their party politics and blank invective;
And we thought the dark
 Women who dyed their hair should have it dyed
  more often.
And we sat in trains all night
 With the windows shut among civil guards and
  peasants
And tried to play piquet by a tiny light
 And tried to sleep bolt upright;
And cursed the Spanish rain
 And cursed their cigarettes which came to pieces
And caught heavy colds in Cordova and in vain
 Waited for the right light for taking photos.
And we met a Cambridge don who said with an air
 'There's going to be trouble shortly in this country',
And ordered anis, pudgy and debonair,
 Glad to show off his mastery of the language.
But only an inch behind

This map of olive and ilex, this painted hoarding,
Careless of visitors the people's mind
    Was tunnelling like a mole to day and danger.
And the day before we left
    We saw the mob in flower at Algeciras
Outside a toothless door, a church bereft
    Of its images and its aura.
And at La Linea while
    The night put miles between us and Gibraltar
We heard the blood-lust of a drunkard pile
    His heaven high with curses;
And next day took the boat
    For home, forgetting Spain, not realizing
That Spain would soon denote
    Our grief, our aspirations;
Not knowing that our blunt
    Ideals would find their whetstones, that our spirit
Would find its frontier on the Spanish front,
    Its body in a rag-tag army.

*The poet Louis MacNeice visited Spain and wrote poems
and articles for journals like* The Spectator. *"Canto VI" is
from* Autumn Journal *(1939).*

ERNEST HEMINGWAY

The Butterfly and the Tank

On this evening I was walking home from the censorship office to the Florida Hotel and it was raining. So
about halfway home I got sick of the rain and stopped
into Chicote's for a quick one. It was the second winter
of shelling in the siege of Madrid and everything was
short including tobacco and people's tempers and you
were a little hungry all the time and would become
suddenly and unreasonably irritated at things you could
do nothing about such as the weather. I should have
gone on home. It was only five blocks more, but when
I saw Chicote's doorway I thought I would get a quick
one and then do those six blocks up the Gran Via
through the mud and rubble of the streets broken by
the bombardment.

The place was crowded. You couldn't get near the bar
and all the tables were full. It was full of smoke, singing, men in uniform, and the smell of wet leather coats,
and they were handing drinks over a crowd that was
three deep at the bar.

A waiter I knew found a chair from another table and I sat down with a thin, white-faced, Adam's-appled German I knew who was working at the censorship and two other people I did not know. The table was in the middle of the room a little on your right as you go in.

You couldn't hear yourself talk for the singing and I ordered a gin and angostura and put it down against the rain. The place was really packed and everybody was very jolly; maybe getting just a little bit too jolly from the newly made Catalan liquor most of them were drinking. A couple of people I did not know slapped me on the back and when the girl at our table said something to me, I couldn't hear it and said, "Sure."

She was pretty terrible looking now I had stopped looking around and was looking at our table; really pretty terrible. But it turned out, when the waiter came, that what she had asked me was to have a drink. The fellow with her was not very forceful looking but she was forceful enough for both of them. She had one of those strong, semi-classical faces and was built like a lion tamer; and the boy with her looked as though he ought to be wearing an old school tie. He wasn't though. He was wearing a leather coat just like all the rest of us. Only it wasn't wet because they had been there since before the rain started. She had on a leather coat too and it was becoming to the sort of face she had.

By this time I was wishing I had not stopped into Chicote's but had gone straight home where you could change your clothes and be dry and have a drink in comfort on the bed with your feet up, and I was tired of looking at both of these young people. Life is very short and ugly women are very long and sitting there at the table I decided that even though I was a writer and supposed to have an insatiable curiosity about all sorts of people, I did not really care to know whether these two were married, or what they saw in each other, or what their politics were, or whether he had a little money, or she had a little money, or anything about them. I decided they must be in the radio. Any time you saw really strange looking civilians in Madrid they were always in the radio. So to say something I raised my voice above the noise and asked, "You in the radio?"

"We are," the girl said. So that was that. They were in the radio.

"How are you comrade?" I said to the German.

"Fine. And you?"

"Wet," I said, and he laughed with his head on one side.

"You haven't got a cigarette?" he asked. I handed him my next to the last pack of cigarettes and he took two. The forceful girl took two and the young man with the old school tie face took one.

"Take another," I shouted.

"No thanks," he answered and the German took it instead.

"Do you mind?" he smiled.

"Of course not," I said. I really minded and he knew it. But he wanted the cigarettes so badly that it did not matter. The singing had died down momentarily, or there was a break in it as there is sometimes in a storm, and we could all hear what we said.

"You been here long?" the forceful girl asked me. She pronounced it bean as in bean soup.

"Off and on," I said.

"We must have a serious talk," the German said. "I want to have a talk with you. When can we have it?"

"I'll call you up," I said. This German was a very strange German indeed and none of the good Germans

liked him. He lived under the delusion that he could
play the piano, but if you kept him away from pianos
he was all right unless he was exposed to liquor, or the
opportunity to gossip, and nobody had even been able
to keep him away from those two things yet.

Gossip was the best thing he did and he always knew
something new and highly discreditable about anyone
you could mention in Madrid, Valencia, Barcelona, and
other political centers.

Just then the singing really started in again, and you
cannot gossip very well shouting, so it looked like a
dull afternoon at Chicote's and I decided to leave as
soon as I should have bought a round myself.

Just then it started. A civilian in a brown suit, a
white shirt, black tie, his hair brushed straight back
from a rather high forehead, who had been clowning
around from table to table, squirted one of the waiters
with a flit gun. Everybody laughed except the waiter
who was carrying a tray full of drinks at the time. He
was indignant.

"*No hay derecho,*" the waiter said. This means, "You
have no right to do that," and is the simplest and the
strongest protest in Spain.

The flit gun man, delighted with his success, and not
seeming to give any importance to the fact that it was
well into the second year of the war, that he was in a
city under siege where everyone was under a strain, and
that he was one of only four men in civilian clothes in
the place, now squirted another waiter.

I looked around for a place to duck to. This waiter,
also, was indignant and the flit gun man squirted him
twice more, lightheartedly. Some people still thought it
was funny, including the forceful girl. But the waiter
stood, shaking his head. His lips were trembling. He

was an old man and he had worked in Chicote's for ten years that I knew of.

"No hay derecho," he said with dignity.

People had laughed, however, and the flit gun man, not noticing how the singing had fallen off, squirted his flit gun at the back of a waiter's neck. The waiter turned, holding his tray.

"No hay derecho," he said. This time it was no protest. It was an indictment and I saw three men in uniform start from a table for the flit gun man and the next thing all four of them were going out the revolving door in a rush and you heard a smack when someone hit the flit gun man on the mouth. Somebody else picked up the flit gun and threw it out the door after him.

The three men came back in looking serious, tough and very righteous. Then the door revolved and in came the flit gun man. His hair was down in his eyes, there was blood on his face, his necktie was pulled to one side and his shirt was torn open. He had the flit gun again and as he pushed, wild-eyed and white-faced, into the room he made one general, unaimed, challenging squirt with it, holding it toward the whole company.

I saw one of the three men start for him and I saw this man's face. There were more men with him now and they forced the flit gun man back between two tables on the left of the room as you go in, the flit gun man struggling wildly now, and when the shot went off I grabbed the forceful girl by the arm and dove for the kitchen door.

The kitchen door was shut and when I put my shoulder against it it did not give.

"Get down here behind the angle of the bar," I said. She knelt there.

"Flat," I said and pushed her down. She was furious.

Every man in the room except the German, who lay behind a table, and the public-school-looking boy who stood in a corner drawn up against the wall, had a gun out. On a bench along the wall three over-blonde girls, their hair dark at the roots, were standing on tiptoe to see and screaming steadily.

"I'm not afraid," the forceful one said. "This is ridiculous."

"You don't want to get shot in a café brawl," I said. "If that flit king has any friends here this can be very bad."

But he had no friends, evidently, because people began putting their pistols away and somebody lifted down the blonde screamers and everyone who had started over there when the shot came, drew back away from the flit man who lay, quietly, on his back on the floor.

"No one is to leave until the police come," someone shouted from the door.

Two policemen with rifles, who had come in off the street patrol, were standing by the door and at this announcement I saw six men form up just like the line-up of a football team coming out of a huddle and head out through the door. Three of them were the men who had first thrown the flit king out. One of them was the man who shot him. They went right through the policemen with the rifles like good interference taking out an end and a tackle. And as they went out one of the policemen got his rifle across the door and shouted, "No one can leave. Absolutely no one."

"Why did those men go? Why hold us if anyone's gone?"

"They were mechanics who had to return to their air field," someone said.

"But if anyone's gone it's silly to hold the others."

"Everyone must wait for the Seguridad. Things must be done legally and in order."

"But don't you see that if any person has gone it is silly to hold the others?"

"No one can leave. Everyone must wait."

"It's comic," I said to the forceful girl.

"No it's not. It's simply horrible."

We were standing up now and she was staring indignantly at where the flit king was lying. His arms were spread wide and he had one leg drawn up.

"I'm going over to help that poor wounded man. Why has no one helped him or done anything for him?"

"I'd leave him alone," I said. "You want to keep out of this."

"But it's simply inhuman. I've nurse's training and I'm going to give him first aid."

"I wouldn't," I said. "Don't go near him."

"Why not?" She was very upset and almost hysterical.

"Because he's dead," I said.

When the police came they held everybody there for three hours. They commenced by smelling of all the pistols. In this manner they would detect one which had been fired recently. After about forty pistols they seemed to get bored with this and anyway all you could smell was wet leather coats. Then they sat at a table placed directly behind the late flit king, who lay on the floor looking like a grey wax caricature of himself, with grey wax hands and a grey wax face, and examined people's papers.

With his shirt ripped open you could see the flit king had no undershirt and the soles of his shoes were worn through. He looked very small and pitiful lying there on the floor. You had to step over him to get to the table where two plain clothes policemen sat and examined everyone's identification papers. The husband lost and found his papers several times with nervousness. He had a safe conduct pass somewhere but he had mislaid it in a pocket but he kept on searching and perspiring until he found it. Then he would put it in a different pocket and have to go searching again. He perspired heavily while doing this and it made his hair very curly and his face red. He now looked as though he should have not only an old school tie but one of those little caps boys in the lower forms wear. You have heard how events age people. Well this shooting had made him look about ten years younger.

While we were waiting around I told the forceful girl I thought the whole thing was a pretty good story and that I would write it sometime. The way the six had lined up in single file and rushed that door was very impressive. She was shocked and said that I could not write it because it would be prejudicial to the cause of the Spanish Republic. I said that I had been in Spain for a long time and that they used to have a phenomenal number of shootings in the old days around Valencia under the monarchy, and that for hundreds of years before the Republic people had been cutting each other with large knives called Navajas in Andalucia, and that if I saw a comic shooting in Chicote's during the war I could write about it just as though it had been in New York, Chicago, Key West or Marseilles. It did not have anything to do with politics. She said I shouldn't. Probably a lot of other people will say I shouldn't too. The German seemed to think it was a pretty good story however, and I gave him the last of the Camels. Well, anyway, finally, after about three hours the police said we could go.

They were sort of worried about me at the Florida because in those days, with the shelling, if you started for home on foot and didn't get there after the bars were closed at seven-thirty, people worried. I was glad to get home and I told the story while we were cooking supper on an electric stove and it had quite a success.

Well, it stopped raining during the night, and the next morning it was a fine, bright, cold early winter day and at twelve forty-five I pushed open the revolving doors at Chicote's to try a little gin and tonic before lunch. There were very few people there at that hour and two waiters and the manager came over to the table. They were all smiling.

"Did they catch the murderer?" I asked.

"Don't make jokes so early in the day," the manager said. "Did *you* see him shot?"

"Yes," I told him.

"Me too," he said. "I was just here when it happened." He pointed to a corner table. "He placed the pistol right against the man's chest when he fired."

"How late did they hold people?"

"Oh until past two this morning."

"They only came for the *fiambre*," using the Spanish slang word for corpse, the same used on menus for cold meat, "at eleven o'clock this morning."

"But you don't know about it yet," the manager said.

"No. He doesn't know," a waiter said.

"It is a very rare thing," another waiter said. *"Muy raro."*

"And sad too," the manager said. He shook his head.

"Yes. Sad and curious," the waiter said. "Very sad."

"Tell me."

"It is a very rare thing," the manager said.

"Tell me. Come on tell me."

45

The manager leaned over the table in great confidence.

"In the flit gun, you know," he said. "He had *eau de cologne*. Poor fellow."

"It was not a joke in such bad taste, you see?" the waiter said.

"It was really just gaiety. No one should have taken offense," the manager said. "Poor fellow."

"I see," I said. "He just wanted everyone to have a good time."

"Yes," said the manager. "It was really just an unfortunate misunderstanding."

"And what about the flit gun?"

"The police took it. They have sent it around to his family."

"I imagine they will be glad to have it," I said.

"Yes," said the manager. "Certainly. A flit gun is always useful."

"Who was he?"

" A cabinet maker."

"Married?"

"Yes, the wife was here with the police this morning."

"What did she say?"

"She dropped down by him and said, 'Pedro, what have they done to thee, Pedro? Who has done this to thee? Oh Pedro.' "

"Then the police had to take her away because she could not control herself," the waiter said.

"It seems he was feeble of the chest," the manager said. "He fought in the first days of the movement. They said he fought in the Sierra but he was too weak in the chest to continue."

"And yesterday afternoon he just went out on the town to cheer things up," I suggested.

"No," said the manager. "You see it is very rare. Everything is *muy raro*. This I learn from the police who are very efficient if given time. They have interrogated comrades from the shop where he worked. This they located from the card of his syndicate which was in his pocket. Yesterday he bought the flit gun and *agua de colonia* to use for a joke at a wedding. He had announced this intention. He bought them across the street. There was a label on the cologne bottle with the address. The bottle was in the washroom. It was there he filled the flit gun. After buying them he must have come in here when the rain started."

"I remember when he came in," a waiter said.

"In the gaiety, with the singing, he became gay too."

"He was gay all right," I said. "He was practically floating around."

The manager kept on with the relentless Spanish logic.

"That is the gaiety of drinking with a weakness of the chest," he said.

"I don't like this story very well," I said.

"Listen," said the manager. "How rare it is. His gaiety comes in contact with the seriousness of the war like a butterfly—"

"Oh very like a butterfly," I said. "Too much like a butterfly."

"I am not joking," said the manager. "You see it? Like a butterfly and a tank."

This pleased him enormously. He was getting into the real Spanish metaphysics.

"Have a drink on the house," he said. "You must write a story about this."

I remembered the flit gun man with his grey wax hands and his grey wax face, his arms spread wide and his legs drawn up and he did look a little like a butterfly; not too much, you know. But he did not look very human either. He reminded me more of a dead sparrow.

"I'll take gin and Schweppes quinine tonic water," I said.

"You must write a story about it," the manager said. "Here. Here's luck."

"Luck," I said. "Look, an English girl last night told me I shouldn't write about it. That it would be very bad for the cause."

"What nonsense," the manager said. "It is very interesting and important, the misunderstood gaiety coming in contact with the deadly seriousness that is here always. To me it is the rarest and most interesting thing which I have seen for some time. You must write it."

"All right," I said. "Sure. Has he any children?"

"No," he said. "I asked the police. But you must write it and you must call it The Butterfly and the Tank."

"All right," I said. "Sure. But I don't like the title much."

"The title is very elegant," the manager said. "It is pure literature."

"All right," I said. "Sure. That's what we'll call it. The Butterfly and the Tank."

And I sat there on that bright cheerful morning, the place smelling clean and newly aired and swept, with the manager who was an old friend and who was now very pleased with the literature we were making together and I took a sip of the gin and tonic water and looked out the sandbagged window and thought of the wife kneeling there and saying, "Pedro. *Pedro*, who has done this to thee, Pedro?" And I thought that the police would never be able to tell her that even if they had the name of the man who pulled the trigger.

Ernest Hemingway was in Spain as a correspondent for the North American Newspaper Alliance. He was also filming the war documentary The Spanish Earth. *Many of Hemingway's stories and novels are set in Spain during the war. "The Butterfly and the Tank" first appeared in* Esquire *in 1938.*

PABLO PICASSO

Address to the American Artists'
Congress

I am sorry I cannot speak to the American Artists' Congress in person, as was my wish, so that I might assure the artists of America, as director of the Prado Museum, that the democratic government of the Spanish Republic has taken all the necessary measures to protect the artistic treasures of Spain during this cruel and unjust war. While the Rebel planes have dropped incendiary bombs on our museums, the people and the militia, at the risk of their lives, have rescued the works of art and placed them in security.

It is my wish at this time to remind you that I have always believed, and still believe, that artists who live and work with spiritual values cannot and should not remain indifferent to a conflict in which the highest values of humanity and civilization are at stake.

Pablo Picasso articulated his opposition to Fascism in interviews, speeches, and paintings (The Dream and Lie of Gen-

eral Franco, Guernica). *He has said, "My work is never symbolic, only the* Guernica *is symbolic. . . . The mural is for the definite expression and solution of a problem and that is why I used symbolism." The preceding speech is Picasso's address to the American Artists' Congress. It originally appeared in* The New York Times, *December 18, 1937.*

WILLIAM CARLOS WILLIAMS

Federico García Lorca

In 1936 Lorca was dragged through the streets of Granada to face the Fascist firing squad. The reasons were not obvious. He was not active in leftist circles; but he was a power—he was a man of the people. His books were burned. . . .

Federico García Lorca, born in 1899 in the vicinity of Granada, produced a number of outstanding works in lyric poetry, drama, and prose between his eighteenth year and the time of his death in 1936 at the age of thirty-seven. He was a pianist, the organizer of a dramatic troupe, and a distinguished folklorist of Spanish popular songs of great distinction.

Many stories are told of him. He was loved by the people. His murder by the Fascist firing squad in Granada is perhaps as he would have wished it to be: to die on the horns of the bull—if a man does not put his sword first through its heart. Like most men of genius he went about little recognized during his life but he has left us a weapon by which to defend our thought and our beliefs, a modern faith which though it may still be little more than vaguely sensed in the rest of the world is awake today in old Spain, in proud defiance of destruction there. By that Lorca lives.

The William Carlos Williams excerpt originally appeared in The Kenyon Review *in 1939.*

FEDERICO GARCÍA LORCA

Lament for Ignacio Sanchez Mejias

1. COGIDA AND DEATH

At five in the afternoon.
It was exactly five in the afternoon.
A boy brought the white sheet
at five in the afternoon.
A frail of lime ready prepared
at five in the afternoon.

The rest was death, and death alone
at five in the afternoon.

The wind carried away the cottonwool
at five in the afternoon.
And the oxide scattered crystal and nickel
at five in the afternoon.
Now the dove and the leopard wrestle
at five in the afternoon.
And a thigh with a desolate horn
at five in the afternoon.

The bass-string struck up
at five in the afternoon.
Arsenic bells and smoke
at five in the afternoon.
Groups of silence in the corners
at five in the afternoon.
And the bull alone with a high heart!
At five in the afternoon.
When the sweat of snow was coming
at five in the afternoon,
when the bull ring was covered in iodine
at five in the afternoon,
death laid eggs in the wound
at five in the afternoon.
At five in the afternoon.
Exactly at five o'clock in the afternoon.

A coffin on wheels is his bed
at five in the afternoon.
Bones and flutes resound in his ears
at five in the afternoon.
Now the bull was bellowing through his forehead
at five in the afternoon.
The room was iridescent with agony
at five in the afternoon.
In the distance the gangrene now comes
at five in the afternoon.
Horn of the lily through green groins
at five in the afternoon.
The wounds were burning like suns
at five in the afternoon,
and the crowd was breaking the windows
at five in the afternoon.
At five in the afternoon.

Ah, that fatal five in the afternoon!
It was five by all the clocks!
It was five in the shade of the afternoon!

2. THE SPILLED BLOOD

I will not see it!

Tell the moon to come
for I do not want to see the blood
of Ignacio on the sand.

I will not see it!

The moon wide open.
Horse of still clouds,
and the grey bull ring of dreams
with willow in the barreras.

I will not see it!

Let my memory kindle!
Warn the jasmines
of such minute whiteness!

I will not see it!

The cow of the ancient world
passed her sad tongue
over a snout of blood
spilled on the sand,
and the bulls of Guisando,

partly death and partly stone,
bellowed like two centuries
sated with treading the earth.
No.
I do not want to see it!
I will not see it!

Ignacio goes up the tiers
with all his death on his shoulders.
He sought for the dawn
but the dawn was no more.
He seeks for his confident profile
and the dream bewilders him.
He sought for his beautiful body
and encountered his opened blood.
I will not see it!
I do not want to hear it spurt
each time with less strength:
that spurt that illuminates
the tiers of seats, and spills
over the corduroy and the leather
of a thirsty multitude.
Who shouts that I should come near!
Do not ask me to see it!

His eyes did not close
when he saw the horns near,
but the terrible mothers
lifted their heads.
And across the ranches,
an air of secret voices rose,
shouting to celestial bulls,
herdsmen of pale mist.
There was no prince in Seville

who could compare with him,
nor sword like his sword
nor heart so true.
Like a river of lions
was his marvellous strength,
and like a marble torso
his firm drawn moderation.
The air of Andalusian Rome
gilded his head
where his smile was a spikenard
of wit and intelligence.
What a great torero in the ring!
What a good peasant in the sierra!
How gentle with the sheaves!
How hard with the spurs!
How tender with the dew!
How dazzling in the fiesta!
How tremendous with the final
banderillas of darkness!

But now he sleeps without end.
Now the moss and the grass
open with sure fingers
the flower of his skull.
And now his blood comes out singing;
singing along marshes and meadows,
sliding on frozen horns,
faltering soulless in the mist,
stumbling over a thousand hoofs
like a long, dark, sad tongue,
to form a pool of agony
close to the starry Guadalquivir.
Oh, white wall of Spain!
Oh, black bull of sorrow!

Oh, hard blood of Ignacio!
Oh, nightingale of his veins!
No.
I will not see it!
No chalice can contain it,
no swallows can drink it,
no frost of light can cool it,
nor song nor deluge of white lilies,
no glass can cover it with silver.
No.
I will not see it!

3. THE LAID OUT BODY

Stone is a forehead where dreams grieve
without curving waters and frozen cypresses.
Stone is a shoulder on which to bear Time
with trees formed of tears and ribbons and planets.

I have seen grey showers move towards the waves
raising their tender riddled arms,
to avoid being caught by the lying stone
which loosens their limbs without soaking the blood.

For stone gathers seed and clouds,
skeleton larks and wolves of penumbra:
but yields not sounds nor crystals nor fire,
only bull rings and bull rings and more bull rings
    without walls.

Now, Ignacio the well born lies on the stone.
All is finished. What is happening? Contemplate his face:

death has covered him with pale sulphur
and has placed on him the head of a dark minotaur.

All is finished. The rain penetrates his mouth.
The air, as if mad, leaves his sunken chest,
and Love, soaked through with tears of snow,
warms itself on the peak of the herd.

What are they saying? A stenching silence settles down.
We are here with a body laid out which fades away,
with a pure shape which had nightingales
and we see it being filled with depthless holes.

Who creases the shroud? What he says is not true!
Nobody sings here, nobody weeps in the corner,
nobody pricks the spurs, nor terrifies the serpent.
Here I want nothing else but the round eyes
to see this body without a chance of rest.

Here I want to see those men of hard voice.
Those that break horses and dominate rivers;
those men of sonorous skeleton who sing
with a mouth full of sun and flint.

Here I want to see them. Before the stone.
Before this body with broken reins.
I want to know from them the way out
for this captain strapped down by death.

I want them to show me a lament like a river
which will have sweet mists and deep shores,
to take the body of Ignacio where it loses itself
without hearing the double panting of the bulls.

Loses itself in the round bull ring of the moon
which feigns in its youth a sad quiet bull:
loses itself in the night without song of fishes
and in the white thicket of frozen smoke.

I don't want them to cover his face with handkerchiefs
that he may get used to the death he carries.
Go, Ignacio; feel not the hot bellowing.
Sleep, fly, rest: even the sea dies!

4. ABSENT SOUL

The bull does not know you, nor the fig tree,
nor the horses, nor the ants in your own house.
The child and the afternoon do not know you
because you have died for ever.

The back of the stone does not know you,
nor the black satin in which you crumble.
Your silent memory does not know you
because you have died for ever.

The autumn will come with small white snails,
misty grapes and with clustered hills,
but no one will look into your eyes
because you have died for ever.

Because you have died for ever,
like all the dead of the Earth,
like all the dead who are forgotten
in a heap of lifeless dogs.

Nobody knows you. No. But I sing of you.
For posterity I sing of your profile and grace.
Of the signal maturity of your understanding.
Of your appetite for death and the taste of its mouth.
Of the sadness of your once valiant gaiety.

It will be a long time, if ever, before there is born
an Andalusian so true, so rich in adventure.
I sing of his elegance with words that groan,
and I remember a sad breeze through the olive trees.

Federico García Lorca, widely acknowledged as the fore-most Spanish poet of his time, was killed by the Fascists in his hometown of Granada on August 19, 1936. His body was never found. "Lament for Ignacio Sánchez Mejías" was his last long poem (1935). The translation here is by Stephen Spender and J. L. Gili.

THOMAS MANN

Spain

Whose affair is it, if not the creative artist's—the man whose emotions are free—to assert the human conscience against the baseness of interest, at once so presumptuous and so petty; to protest against the stultifying, all-embracing confusion made in our time between politics and villainy?

There is no lower kind of scorn than that visited upon the artist who "descends into the arena". And the ground of that scorn is interest: interest which prefers to gain its ends in darkness and silence, unchecked by the forces of the intellect or the spirit. These, interest would confine to their proper domain of the cultural, by telling them that politics is beneath their dignity. The result is that the cultural becomes the slave of interest, its accessory and accomplice, all for the false coin of a little dignity in return. The artist must not see, that in this stately retreat to his ivory tower he is committing an act of anachronistic folly—must not see, yet to-day can hardly fail to see.

Democracy is to-day to that extent a realised and intrinsic fact, that politics is everybody's business. Nobody can deny this; it stares us in the face with an immediacy never known before. Sometimes we hear somebody say: "I take no interest in politics." The words strike us as absurd. Not only so, but egotistic and antisocial, a stupid self-deception, a piece of folly. But they are more: they betray an ignorance not only intellectual but ethical. For the politico-social field is an undeniable and inalienable part of the all-embracing human; it is one section of the human problem, the human *task*, which the non-political man thinks to set off, as the decisive and actual, against the political sphere. The decisive and the actual: it is indeed that; for in the guise of the political the problem of the human being, man himself, is put to us to-day with a final, life-and-death seriousness unknown before. Then shall the artist—he who, by nature and destiny, ever occupies humanity's furthest outposts —shall he alone be allowed to shirk a decision?

Life-and-death seriousness. I use these words to express the conviction that a man's—and how much more an artist's—opinions are to-day bound up with the salvation of his soul. I deliberately use a religious terminology; so convinced am I, that an artist who, in our time avoids the issue, shirks the human problem when politically presented, and betrays to interest the things of the spirit, is a lost soul. He must be stunted. Not only because he sacrifices his existence as an artist, his "talent", and produces nothing more which is available for life. But because even his earlier work, not created under the pressure of such guilt, and once good, will cease to be good and crumble to dust before humanity's eyes. That is my conviction. I have instances in mind as I write.

I shall be asked what I mean by spirit and what by interest. Well then: the spiritual, seen from the politico-social angle, is the longing of the people for better, juster, happier conditions of life, more adequate to the developed human consciousness. It is this longing, affirmed by all those who are of good will. And interest: interest is all that which seeks to thwart this consummation, because it would thereby be cut off from certain advantages and privileges; seeks by every means at its command, not scorning the basest, even the criminal. Or, well knowing that in the long run it must fail, tries to put off as long as it can the evil day—for a little while, for a few decades. In Spain, interest rages. Rages with a shamelessness such as the world has seldom seen. What has been happening there for many months is one of the most scandalous and mortifying pages which history has to show. Does the world see it, feel it? Only very partially. For murderous interest understands only too well how to besot the world and throw dust in its eyes. From a lady—living, it is true, in the most darkened quarter of the world, I mean Germany—I have heard the words: "Who could have thought that the Reds in Spain would commit such atrocities, out of a blue sky?" The Reds. And out of a blue sky.—The present book, written not by savage Bolsheviks but by persons of Christian and middle-class views, shows how little revolutionary was the reform programme of the Spanish Popular Front, a political alliance of republicans and socialists. It shows us to what circumstances and conditions its legitimate and decisive triumph at the polls was the answer. Have we then no hearts? No understanding? Shall we let ourselves be unresistingly deprived of our last remnant of free human judgment by interest—which unfailingly appeals to the worst instincts, though it clothe itself in lying names such as order, culture, God, and native land? A people held down and exploited with all the instruments of the most obsolete reaction, strives towards a brighter existence, more compatible with human dignity, a social order more creditable to the face of civilisation. Freedom and progress are there conceptions not yet vitiated by philosophical irony and scepticism. For these people they are conditions of national honour, values to be striven for to the uttermost. The government, with all the caution prescribed by the special circumstances, undertakes to remove the grossest abuses, to carry out the most imperative reforms. What happens? An insurrection of generals, occurring in the interest of the old exploiters and oppressors, concocted with the help of hopeful foreign interests, blazes up and misfires. It is already as good as beaten, when it is propped up by foreign governments inimical to freedom, in return for promises of strategic and economic advantage in case of victory. It is supported by money, men, and material, fostered and prolonged, until there seems no end to the bloodshed, the tragic, ruthless, obstinate carnage from either side. Against a people desperately fighting for its freedom and its human rights the troops of its own colony are led into battle. Its cities are demolished by foreign bombing planes, women and children are butchered; and all this is called a national movement; this villainy crying out to heaven is called God, Order, and Beauty. If the interested European Press could have its way, the capital would have fallen long since; the triumph of Order and Beauty over the Marxist rabble would long since have been consummated. But the half-demolished capital—at least at the moment of writing—is not yet conquered, and the "Red mob", as the interested Press describes it, referring to the Spanish people, is defending its life, its higher life, with a lion-like courage which must give to think even the most besotted slave of interest, as to the moral forces here engaged.

The right of self-determination of peoples enjoys high official honour throughout the world to-day. Even our dictators and our totalitarian states lay stress upon it, finding it important to show that they have ninety to ninety-eight per cent of their people behind them. Well, so much is clear: the revolting military have not got the Spanish people behind them, and cannot pretend that they have. They must do their best with Moors and foreign troops. It may not be quite settled what the Spanish people want. But what they do not want is clear, abundantly: General Franco. Those European governments which are interested in the strangulation of freedom, have recognized as legal the rebel junta, in the midst of a furious struggle which they support even if they did not connive at its inception. At home they betray a considerable degree of sensitiveness in the matter of high treason. Here they support a man who delivers up his country to the foreigner. At home they call themselves nationalists. Here they enforce the power of a man to whom his country's independence is naught, if he can do to death freedom and the rights of human-ity; who declares that rather shall two-thirds of the Spanish people die than that Marxism—that is to say a better, juster, more humane order—shall triumph. It is all too infuriating, criminal, and revolting.

Thomas Mann contributed this essay for a pamphlet pub-lished by the Socialist Alliance of Swiss Women in Zurich, 1936. The translation here is by H. T. Lowe-Porter.

ANTOINE DE SAINT-EXUPÉRY

Barcelona and Madrid

Machine-gun bullets cracked against the stone above our heads as we skirted the moonlit wall. Low-flying lead thudded into the rubble of an embankment that rose on the other side of the road. Half a mile away a battle was in progress, the lines of fire drawn in the shape of a horse-shoe ahead of us and on our flanks.

Walking between wall and parapet on the white highway, my guide and I were able to disregard the spatter of missiles in a feeling of perfect security. We could sing, we could laugh, we could strike matches, without drawing upon ourselves the direct fire of the enemy. We went forward like peasants on their way to market. Half a mile away the iron hand of war would have set us inescapably upon the black chessboard of battle; but here, out of the game, ignored, the Republican lieutenant and I were as free as air.

Shells filled the night with absurd parabolas during their three seconds of freedom between release and exhaustion. There were the duds that dove without bursting into the ground; there were the travelers in space that whipped straight overhead, elongated in their race to the stars. And the leaden bullets that ricocheted in our faces and tinkled curiously in our ears were like bees, dangerous for the twinkling of an eye, poisonous but ephemeral.

Walking on, we reached a point where the embankment had collapsed.

"We might follow the cross-trench from here," my guide suggested.

Things had suddenly turned serious. Not that we were in the line of machine-gun fire, or that a roving searchlight was about to spot us. It was not as bad as that. There had simply been a rustling overhead; a sort of celestial gurgle had sounded. It meant no harm to us, but the lieutenant remarked suddenly, "That is meant for Madrid," and we went down into the trench.

The trench ran along the crest of a hill a little before reaching the suburb of Carabanchel. In the direction of Madrid a part of the parapet had crumbled and we could see the city in the gap, white, strangely white, under the full moon. Hardly a mile separated us from those tall structures dominated by the tower of the Telephone Building.

Madrid was asleep—or rather Madrid was feigning sleep. Not a light; not a sound. Like clockwork, every two minutes the funereal fracas that we were henceforth to hear roared forth and was dissolved in a dead silence. It seemed to waken no sound and no stirring in the city, but was swallowed up each time like a stone in water.

Suddenly in the place of Madrid I felt that I was

staring at a face with closed eyes. The hard face of an obstinate virgin taking blow after blow without a moan. Once again there sounded overhead that gurgling in the stars of a newly uncorked bottle. One second, two seconds, five seconds went by. There was an explosion and I ducked involuntarily. There goes the whole town, I thought.

But Madrid was still there. Nothing had collapsed. Not an eye had blinked. Nothing was changed. The stone face was as pure as ever.

"Meant for Madrid," the lieutenant repeated mechanically. He taught me to tell these celestial shudders apart, to follow the course of these sharks rushing upon their prey:

"No, that is one of our batteries replying. . . . That's theirs, but firing somewhere else. . . . There's one meant for Madrid."

Waiting for an explosion is the longest passage of time I know. What things go on in that interminable moment! An enormous pressure rises, rises. Will that boiler ever make up its mind to burst? At last! For some that meant death, but there are others for whom it meant escape from death. Eight hundred thousand souls, less half a score of dead, have won a last-minute reprieve. Between the gurgling and the explosion eight hundred thousand lives were in danger of death.

Each shell in the air threatened them all. I could feel the city out there, tense, compact, a solid. I saw them all in the mind's eye—men, women, children, all that humble population crouching in the sheltering cloak of stone of a motionless virgin. Again I heard the ignoble crash and was gripped and sickened by the downward course of the torpedo. . . . Torpedo? I scarcely knew what I was saying. "They . . . they are torpedoing Madrid." And the lieutenant, standing there counting the shells, said:

"Meant for Madrid. Sixteen."

I crept out of the trench, lay flat on my stomach on the parapet, and stared. A new image has wiped out the old. Madrid with its chimney-pots, its towers, its port-holes, now looks like a ship on the high seas. Madrid all white on the black waters of the night. A city out-lives its inhabitants. Madrid, loaded with emigrants, is ferrying them from one shore to the other of life. It has a generation on board. Slowly it navigates through the centuries. Men, women, children fill it from garret to hold. Resigned or quaking with fear, they live only for the moment to come. A vessel loaded with humanity is being torpedoed. The purpose of the enemy is to sink Madrid as if she were a ship.

Stretched out on the parapet I do not care a curse for the rules of war. For justifications or for motives. I listen. I have learned to read the course of these gur-glings among the stars. They pass quite close to Sagit-tarius. I have learned to count slowly up to five. And I listen. But what tree has been sundered by this light-ning, what cathedral has been gutted, what poor child has just been stricken, I have no means of knowing.

That same afternoon I had witnessed a bombardment in the town itself. All the force of this thunder-clap had to burst on the Gran Via in order to uproot a human life. One single life. Passers-by had brushed rubbish off their clothes; others had scattered on the run; and when the light smoke had risen and cleared away, the be-trothed, escaped by miracle without a scratch, found at his feet his *novia*, whose golden arm a moment before had been in his, changed into a blood-filled sponge, changed into a limp packet of flesh and rags.

He had knelt down, still uncomprehending, had nodded his head slowly, as if saying to himself, "Something very strange has happened."

This marvel spattered on the pavement bore no resemblance to what had been his beloved. Misery was excruciatingly slow to engulf him in its tidal wave. For still another second, stunned by the feat of the invisible prestidigitator, he cast a bewildered glance round him in search of the slender form, as if it at least should have survived. Nothing was there but a packet of muck.

Gone was the feeble spark of humanity. And while in the man's throat there was brewing that shriek which I know not what deferred, he had the leisure to reflect that it was not those lips he had loved but their pout, not them but their smile. Not those eyes, but their glance. Not that breast, but its gentle swell. He was free to discover at last the source of the anguish love had been storing up for him, to learn that it was the unattainable he had been pursuing. What he had yearned to embrace was not the flesh but a downy spirit, a spark, the impalpable angel that inhabits the flesh.

I do not care a curse for the rules of war and the law of reprisal. As for the military advantage of such a bombardment, I simply cannot grasp it. I have seen housewives disemboweled, children mutilated; I have seen the old itinerant market crone sponge from her treasures the brains with which they were spattered. I have seen a janitor's wife come out of her cellar and douse the sullied pavement with a bucket of water, and I am still unable to understand what part these humble slaughterhouse accidents play in warfare.

A moral rôle? But a bombardment turns against the bombarder! Each shell that fell upon Madrid fortified something in the town. It persuaded the hesitant neutral to plump for the defenders. A dead child weighs heavily in the balance when it is one's own. It was clear to me that a bombardment did not disperse—it unified. Horror causes men to clench their fists, and in horror men join together.

The lieutenant and I crawled along the parapet. Face or ship, Madrid stood erect, receiving blows without a moan. But men are like this: slowly but surely, ordeal fortifies their virtues.

Because of the ordeal my companion's heart was high. He was thinking of the hardening of Madrid's will. He stood up with his fists on his hips, breathing heavily. Pity for the women and the children had gone out of him.

"That makes sixty," he counted grimly.

The blow resounded on the anvil. A giant smith was forging Madrid.

One side or the other would win. Madrid would resist or it would fall. A thousand forces were engaged in this mortal confusion of tongues from which anything might come forth. But one did not need to be a Martian, did not need to see these men dispassionately in a long perspective, in order to perceive that they were struggling against themselves, were their own enemy. Mankind perhaps was being brought to bed of something here in Spain; something perhaps was to be born of this chaos, this disruption. For indeed not all that I saw in Spain was horror, not all of it filled my mouth with a taste of ashes.

The French writer and pilot Antoine de Saint-Exupéry flew into Barcelona in 1936. As a correspondent for L'Intransigeant, *he made his way to the front—and the bombing of Madrid—with the anarchists. "Barcelona and Madrid" is from his book* Wind, Sand and Stars *(1939).*

GEORGE ORWELL

Homage to Catalonia

One afternoon Benjamin told us that he wanted fifteen volunteers. The attack on the Fascist redoubt which had been called off on the previous occasion was to be carried out tonight. I oiled my ten Mexican cartridges, dirtied my bayonet (the things give your position away if they flash too much), and packed up a hunk of bread, three inches of red sausage, and a cigar which my wife had sent from Barcelona and which I had been hoarding for a long time. Bombs were served out, three to a man. The Spanish Government had at last succeeded in producing a decent bomb. It was on the principle of a Mills bomb, but with two pins instead of one. After you had pulled the pins out there was an interval of seven seconds before the bomb exploded. Its chief disadvantage was that one pin was very stiff and the other very loose, so that you had the choice of leaving both pins in place and being unable to pull the stiff one out in a moment of emergency, or pulling out the stiff one beforehand and being in a constant stew lest the thing should explode in your pocket. But it was a handy little bomb to throw.

A little before midnight Benjamin led the fifteen of us down to Torre Fabian. Ever since evening the rain had been pelting down. The irrigation ditches were brimming over, and every time you stumbled into one you were in water up to your waist. In the pitch darkness and sheeting rain in the farm-yard a dim mass of men was waiting. Kopp addressed us, first in Spanish, then in English, and explained the plan of attack. The Fascist line here made an L-bend and the parapet we were to attack lay on rising ground at the corner of the L. About thirty of us, half English and half Spanish, under the command of Jorge Roca, our battalion commander (a battalion in the militia was about four hundred men), and Benjamin, were to creep up and cut the Fascist wire. Jorge would fling the first bomb as a signal, then the rest of us were to send in a rain of bombs, drive the Fascists out of the parapet and seize it before they could rally. Simultaneously seventy Shock Troopers were to assault the next Fascist 'position,' which lay two hundred yards to the right of the other, joined to it by a communication-trench. To prevent us from shooting each other in the darkness white armlets would be worn. At this moment a messenger arrived to say that there were no white armlets. Out of the darkness a plaintive voice suggested: "Couldn't we arrange for the Fascists to wear white armlets instead?"

There was an hour or two to put in. The barn over the mule stable was so wrecked by shell-fire that you could not move about in it without a light. Half the floor had been torn away by a plunging shell and there was a twenty-foot drop on to the stones beneath. Someone found a pick and levered a burst plank out of the floor, and in a few minutes we had got a fire alight and our drenched clothes were steaming. Someone else produced a pack of cards. A rumour—one of those mysterious rumours that are endemic in war—flew round that hot coffee with brandy in it was about to be served out. We filed eagerly down the almost-collapsing staircase and wandered round the dark yard, enquiring where the coffee was to be found. Alas! there was no coffee. Instead, they called us together, ranged us into single file, and then Jorge and Benjamin set off rapidly into the darkness, the rest of us following.

It was still raining and intensely dark, but the wind had dropped. The mud was unspeakable. The paths through the beet-fields were simply a succession of lumps, as slippery as a greasy pole, with huge pools everywhere. Long before we got to the place where we were to leave our own parapet everyone had fallen several times and our rifles were coated with mud. At the parapet a small knot of men, our reserves, were waiting, and the doctor and a row of stretchers. We filed through the gap in the parapet and waded through another irrigation ditch. Splash-gurgle! Once again in water up to your waist, with the filthy, slimy mud oozing over your boot-tops. On the grass outside Jorge waited till we were all through. Then, bent almost double, he began creeping slowly forward. The Fascist parapet was about a hundred and fifty yards away. Our one chance of getting there was to move without noise.

I was in front with Jorge and Benjamin. Bent double, but with faces raised, we crept into the almost utter darkness at a pace that grew slower at every step. The rain beat lightly in our faces. When I glanced back I could see the men who were nearest to me, a bunch of humped shapes like huge black mushrooms gliding slowly forward. But every time I raised my head Benjamin, close beside me, whispered fiercely in my ear: "To keep ze head down! To keep ze head down!" I could have told him that he needn't worry. I knew by experiment that on a dark night you can never see a man at twenty paces. It was far more important to go quietly. If they once heard us we were done for. They had only to spray the darkness with their machine-gun and there was nothing for it but to run or be massacred.

But on the sodden ground it was almost impossible to move quietly. Do what you would your feet stuck to the mud, and every step you took was slop-slop, slop-slop. And the devil of it was that the wind had dropped, and in spite of the rain it was a very quiet night. Sounds would carry a long way. There was a dreadful moment when I kicked against a tin and thought every Fascist within miles must have heard it. But no, not a sound, no answering shot, no movement in the Fascist lines. We crept onwards, always more slowly. I cannot convey to you the depth of my desire to get there. Just to get within bombing distance before they heard us! At such a time you have not even any fear, only a tremendous hopeless longing to get over the intervening ground. I have felt exactly the same thing when stalking a wild animal; the same agonized desire to get within range, the same dreamlike certainty that it is impossible. And how the distance stretched out! I knew the ground well, it was barely a hundred and fifty yards, and yet it seemed more like a mile. When you are creeping at that pace you are aware as an ant might be of the enormous variations in the ground; the splendid patch of smooth grass here, the evil patch of sticky mud there, the tall rustling reeds that have got to be avoided, the heap of stones that almost makes you give up hope because it seems impossible to get over it without noise.

We had been creeping forward for such an age that I began to think we had gone the wrong way. Then in the darkness thin parallel lines of something blacker were faintly visible. It was the outer wire (the Fascists had two lines of wire). Jorge knelt down, fumbled in his pocket. He had our only pair of wire-cutters. Snip, snip. The trailing stuff was lifted delicately aside. We waited for the men at the back to close up. They seemed to be making a frightful noise. It might be fifty yards to the Fascist parapet now. Still onwards, bent double. A stealthy step, lowering your foot as gently as a cat approaching a mousehole; then a pause to listen; then another step. Once I raised my head; in silence Benjamin put his hand behind my neck and pulled it violently down. I knew that the inner wire was barely twenty yards from the parapet. It seemed to me inconceivable that thirty men could get there unheard. Our breathing was enough to give us away. Yet somehow we did get there. The Fascist parapet was visible now, a dim black mound, looming high above us. Once again Jorge knelt and fumbled. Snip, snip. There was no way of cutting the stuff silently.

So that was the inner wire. We crawled through it on all fours and rather more rapidly. If we had time to deploy now all was well. Jorge and Benjamin crawled across to the right. But the men behind, who were spread out, had to form into single file to get through the narrow gap in the wire, and just at this moment there was a flash and a bang from the Fascist parapet. The sentry had heard us at last. Jorge poised himself on one knee and swung his arm like a bowler. Crash! His bomb burst somewhere over the parapet. At once, far

more promptly than one would have thought possible,
a roar of fire, ten or twenty rifles, burst out from the
Fascist parapet. They had been waiting for us after all.
Momentarily you could see every sandbag in the lurid
light. Men too far back were flinging their bombs and
some of them were falling short of the parapet. Every
loophole seemed to be sprouting jets of flame. It is always hateful to be shot at in the dark—every rifle-flash
seems to be pointed straight at yourself—but it was the
bombs that were the worst. You cannot conceive the
horror of these things till you have seen one burst close
to you and in darkness; in the daytime there is only the
crash of the explosion, in the darkness there is the blind-
ing red glare as well. I had flung myself down at the
first volley. All this while I was lying on my side in the
greasy mud, wrestling savagely with the pin of a bomb.
The damned thing *would* not come out. Finally I
realized that I was twisting it in the wrong direction. I
got the pin out, rose to my knees, hurled the bomb, and
threw myself down again. The bomb burst over to the
right, outside the parapet; fright had spoiled my aim.
Just at this moment another bomb burst right in front
of me, so close that I could feel the heat of the explosion.
I flattened myself out and dug my face into the mud so
hard that I hurt my neck and thought that I was
wounded. Through the din I heard an English voice
behind me say quietly: "I'm hit." The bomb had, in
fact, wounded several people round about me without
touching myself. I rose to my knees and flung my second
bomb. I forget where that one went.

The Fascists were firing, our people behind were
firing, and I was very conscious of being in the middle.
I felt the blast of a shot and realized that a man was
firing from immediately behind me. I stood up and

shouted at him: "Don't shoot at me, you bloody fool!"
At this moment I saw that Benjamin, ten or fifteen yards
to my right, was motioning to me with his arm. I ran
across to him. It meant crossing the line of spouting
loopholes, and as I went I clapped my left hand over my
cheek; an idiotic gesture—as though one's hand could
stop a bullet!—but I had a horror of being hit in the
face. Benjamin was kneeling on one knee with a pleased,
devilish sort of expression on his face and firing carefully at the rifle-flashes with his automatic pistol. Jorge
had dropped wounded at the first volley and was somewhere out of sight. I knelt beside Benjamin, pulled the
pin out of my third bomb and flung it. Ah! No doubt
about it that time. The bomb crashed inside the parapet, at the corner, just by the machine-gun nest.

The Fascist fire seemed to have slackened very suddenly. Benjamin leapt to his feet and shouted: "Forward! Charge!" We dashed up the short steep slope on
which the parapet stood. I say 'dashed'; 'lumbered'
would be a better word; the fact is that you can't move
fast when you are sodden and mudded from head to
foot and weighted down with a heavy rifle and bayonet
and a hundred and fifty cartridges. I took it for granted
that there would be a Fascist waiting for me at the top.
If he fired at that range he could not miss me, and yet
somehow I never expected him to fire, only to try for
me with his bayonet. I seemed to feel in advance the
sensation of our bayonets crossing, and I wondered
whether his arm would be stronger than mine. However,
there was no Fascist waiting. With a vague feeling of
relief I found that it was a low parapet and the sandbags
gave a good foothold. As a rule they are difficult to get
over. Everything inside was smashed to pieces, beams
flung all over the place, and great shards of uralite

littered everywhere. Our bombs had wrecked all the huts and dug-outs. And still there was not a soul visible. I thought they would be lurking somewhere underground, and shouted in English (I could not think of any Spanish at the moment): "Come on out of it! Surrender!" No answer. Then a man, a shadowy figure in the half-light, skipped over the roof of one of the ruined huts and dashed away to the left. I started after him, prodding my bayonet ineffectually into the darkness. As I rounded the corner of the hut I saw a man—I don't know whether or not it was the same man as I had seen before—fleeing up the communication-trench that led to the other Fascist position. I must have been very close to him, for I could see him clearly. He was bareheaded and seemed to have nothing on except a blanket which he was clutching round his shoulders. If I had fired I could have blown him to pieces. But for fear of shooting one another we had been ordered to use only bayonets once we were inside the parapet, and in any case I never even thought of firing. Instead, my mind leapt backwards twenty years, to our boxing instructor at school, showing me in vivid pantomime how he had bayoneted a Turk at the Dardanelles. I gripped my rifle by the small of the butt and lunged at the man's back. He was just out of my reach. Another lunge: still out of reach. And for a little distance we proceeded like this, he rushing up the trench and I after him on the ground above, prodding at his shoulder-blades and never quite getting there—a comic memory for me to look back upon, though I suppose it seemed less comic to him.

Of course, he knew the ground better than I and had soon slipped away from me. When I came back the position was full of shouting men. The noise of firing had lessened somewhat. The Fascists were still pouring a heavy fire at us from three sides, but it was coming from a greater distance. We had driven them back for the time being. I remember saying in an oracular manner: "We can hold this place for half an hour, not more." I don't know why I picked on half an hour. Looking over the right-hand parapet you could see innumerable greenish rifle-flashes stabbing the darkness; but they were a long way back, a hundred or two hundred yards. Our job now was to search the position and loot anything that was worth looting. Benjamin and some others were already scrabbling among the ruins of a big hut or dug-out in the middle of the position. Benjamin staggered excitedly through the ruined roof, tugging at the rope handle of an ammunition box.

"Comrades! Ammunition! Plenty ammunition here!"

"We don't want ammuntion," said a voice, "we want rifles."

This was true. Half our rifles were jammed with mud and unusable. They could be cleaned, but it is dangerous to take the bolt out of a rifle in the darkness; you put it down somewhere and then you lose it. I had a tiny electric torch which my wife had managed to buy in Barcelona, otherwise we had no light of any description among us. A few men with good rifles began a desultory fire at the flashes in the distance. No one dared fire too rapidly; even the best of the rifles were liable to jam if they got too hot. There were about sixteen of us inside the parapet, including one or two who were wounded. A number of wounded, English and Spanish, were lying outside. Patrick O'Hara, a Belfast Irishman who had had some training in first-aid, went to and fro with packets of bandages, binding up the wounded men and, of course, being shot at every time he returned to the parapet, in spite of his indignant shouts of "Poum!"

We began searching the position. There were several dead men lying about, but I did not stop to examine them. The thing I was after was the machine-gun. All the while when we were lying outside I had been wondering vaguely why the gun did not fire. I flashed my torch inside the machine-gun nest. A bitter disappointment! The gun was not there. Its tripod was there, and various boxes of ammunition and spare parts, but the gun was gone. They must have unscrewed it and carried it off at the first alarm. No doubt they were acting under orders, but it was a stupid and cowardly thing to do, for if they had kept the gun in place they could have slaughtered the whole lot of us. We were furious. We had set our hearts on capturing a machine-gun.

We poked here and there but did not find anything of much value. There were quantities of Fascist bombs lying about—a rather inferior type of bomb, which you touched off by pulling a string—and I put a couple of them in my pocket as souvenirs. It was impossible not to be struck by the bare misery of the Fascist dug-outs. The litter of spare clothes, books, food, petty personal belongings that you saw in our own dug-outs was completely absent; these poor unpaid conscripts seemed to own nothing except blankets and a few soggy hunks of bread. Up at the far end there was a small dug-out which was partly above ground and had a tiny window. We flashed the torch through the window and instantly raised a cheer. A cylindrical object in a leather case, four feet high and six inches in diameter, was leaning against the wall. Obviously the machine-gun barrel. We dashed round and got in at the doorway, to find that the thing in the leather case was not a machine-gun but something which, in our weapon-starved army, was even more precious. It was an enormous telescope, probably of at least sixty or seventy magnifications, with a folding tripod. Such telescopes simply did not exist on our side of the line and they were desperately needed. We brought it out in triumph and leaned it against the parapet, to be carried off later.

At this moment someone shouted that the Fascists were closing in. Certainly the din of firing had grown very much louder. But it was obvious that the Fascists would not counter-attack from the right, which meant crossing no man's land and assaulting their own parapet. If they had any sense at all they would come at us from inside the line. I went round to the other side of the dug-outs. The position was roughly horseshoe-shaped, with the dug-outs in the middle, so that we had another parapet covering us on the left. A heavy fire was coming from that direction, but it did not matter greatly. The danger-spot was straight in front, where there was no protection at all. A stream of bullets was passing just overhead. They must be coming from the other Fascist position farther up the line; evidently the Shock Troopers had not captured it after all. But this time the noise was deafening. It was the unbroken, drum-like roar of massed rifles which I was used to hearing from a little distance; this was the first time I had been in the middle of it. And by now, of course, the firing had spread along the line for miles around. Douglas Thompson, with a wounded arm dangling useless at his side, was leaning against the parapet and firing one-handed at the flashes. Someone whose rifle had jammed was loading for him.

There were four or five of us round this side. It was

obvious what we must do. We must drag the sand-bags from the front parapet and make a barricade across the unprotected side. And we had got to be quick. The fire was high at present, but they might lower it at any moment; by the flashes all round I could see that we had a hundred or two hundred men against us. We began wrenching the sand-bags loose, carrying them twenty yards forward and dumping them into a rough heap. It was a vile job. They were big sand-bags, weighing a hundredweight each and it took every ounce of your strength to prise them loose; and then the rotten sacking split and the damp earth cascaded all over you, down your neck and up your sleeves. I remember feeling a deep horror at everything: the chaos, the darkness, the frightful din, the slithering to and fro in the mud, the struggles with the bursting sand-bags—all the time encumbered with my rifle, which I dared not put down for fear of losing it. I even shouted to someone as we staggered along with a bag between us: "This is war! Isn't it bloody?" Suddenly a succession of tall figures came leaping over the front parapet. As they came nearer we saw that they wore the uniform of the Shock Troopers, and we cheered, thinking they were reinforcements. However, there were only four of them, three Germans and a Spaniard. We heard afterwards what had happened to the Shock Troopers. They did not know the ground and in the darkness had been led to the wrong place, where they were caught on the Fascist wire and numbers of them were shot down. These were four who had got lost, luckily for themselves. The Germans did not speak a word of English, French, or Spanish. With difficulty and much gesticulation we explained what we were doing and got them to help us in building the barricade.

The Fascists had brought up a machine-gun now. You could see it spitting like a squib a hundred or two hundred yards away; the bullets came over us with a steady, frosty crackle. Before long we had flung enough sand-bags into place to make a low breastwork behind which the few men who were on this side of the position could lie down and fire. I was kneeling behind them. A mortar-shell whizzed over and crashed somewhere in no man's land. That was another danger, but it would take them some minutes to find our range. Now that we had finished wrestling with those beastly sand-bags it was not bad fun in a way; the noise, the darkness, the flashes approaching, our own men blazing back at the flashes. One even had time to think a little. I remember wondering whether I was frightened, and deciding that I was not. Outside, where I was probably in less danger, I had been half sick with fright. Suddenly there was another shout that the Fascists were closing in. There was no doubt about it this time, the rifle-flashes were much nearer. I saw a flash hardly twenty yards away. Obviously they were working their way up the communication-trench. At twenty yards they were within easy bombing range; there were eight or nine of us bunched together and a single well-placed bomb would blow us all to fragments. Bob Smillie, the blood running down his face from a small wound, sprang to his knee and flung a bomb. We cowered, waiting for the crash. The fuse fizzled red as it sailed through the air, but the bomb failed to explode. (At least a quarter of these bombs were duds.) I had no bombs left except the Fascist ones and I was not certain how these worked. I shouted to the others to know if anyone had a bomb to spare. Douglas Moyle felt in his pocket and passed one across. I flung it and threw myself on my face. By one of those strokes of luck that happen about once in a year I had managed to drop the bomb almost exactly where the rifle had flashed. There was the roar of the explosion and then, instantly, a diabolical outcry of screams and groans. We had got one of them, anyway; I don't know whether he was killed, but certainly he was badly hurt. Poor wretch, poor wretch! I felt a vague sorrow as I heard him screaming. But at the same instant, in the dim light of the rifle-flashes, I saw or thought I saw a figure standing near the place where the rifle had flashed. I threw up my rifle and let fly. Another scream, but I think it was still the effect of the bomb. Several more bombs were thrown. The next rifle-flashes we saw were a long way off, a hundred yards or more. So we had driven them back, temporarily at least.

Everyone began cursing and saying why the hell didn't they send us some supports. With a sub-machine-gun or twenty men with clean rifles we could hold this place against a battalion. At this moment Paddy Donovan, who was second-in-command to Benjamin and had been sent back for orders, climbed over the front parapet.

"Hi! Come on out of it! All men to retire at once!"

"What?"

"Retire! Get out of it!"

"Why?"

"Orders. Back to our own lines double-quick."

People were already climbing over the front parapet. Several of them were struggling with a heavy ammunition box. My mind flew to the telescope which I had left leaning against the parapet on the other side of the position. But at this moment I saw that the four Shock Troopers, acting I suppose on some mysterious orders they had received beforehand, had begun running up the communication-trench. It led to the other Fascist position and—if they got there—to certain death. They were disappearing into the darkness. I ran after them, trying to think of the Spanish for 'retire'; finally I shouted, "Atrás! Atrás!" which perhaps conveyed the right meaning. The Spaniard understood it and brought the others back. Paddy was waiting at the parapet.

"Come on, hurry up."

"But the telescope!"

"B—— the telescope! Benjamin's waiting outside."

We climbed out. Paddy held the wire aside for me. As soon as we got away from the shelter of the Fascist parapet we were under a devilish fire that seemed to be coming at us from every direction. Part of it, I do not doubt, came from our own side, for everyone was firing all along the line. Whichever way we turned a fresh stream of bullets swept past; we were driven this way and that in the darkness like a flock of sheep. It did not make it any easier that we were dragging a captured box of ammunition—one of those boxes that hold 1750 rounds and weigh about a hundredweight—besides a box of bombs and several Fascist rifles. In a few minutes, although the distance from parapet to parapet was not two hundred yards and most of us knew the ground, we were completely lost. We found ourselves slithering about in a muddy field, knowing nothing except that bullets were coming from both sides. There was no moon to go by, but the sky was growing a little lighter. Our lines lay east of Huesca; I wanted to stay where we were till the first crack of dawn showed us which was east and which was west; but the others were against it. We slithered onwards, changing our direction several times and taking it in turns to haul at the ammunition-box. At last we saw the low flat line of a parapet loom-

ing in front of us. It might be ours or it might be the
Fascists'; nobody had the dimmest idea which way we
were going. Benjamin crawled on his belly through some
tall whitish weed till he was about twenty yards from
the parapet and tried a challenge. A shout of "Poum!"
answered him. We jumped to our feet, found our way
along the parapet, slopped once more through the irrigation ditch—splash-gurgle!—and were in safety.

Kopp was waiting inside the parapet with a few
Spaniards. The doctor and the stretchers were gone. It
appeared that all the wounded had been got in except
Jorge and one of our own men, Hiddlestone by name,
who were missing. Kopp was pacing up and down, very
pale. Even the fat folds at the back of his neck were
pale; he was paying no attention to the bullets that
streamed over the low parapet and cracked close to his
head. Most of us were squatting behind the parapet for
cover. Kopp was muttering. "Jorge! Cogno! Jorge!" And
then in English. "If Jorge is gone it is terreeble, terreeble!" Jorge was his personal friend and one of his
best officers. Suddenly he turned to us and asked for five
volunteers, two English and three Spanish, to go and
look for the missing men. Moyle and I volunteered with
three Spaniards.

As we got outside the Spaniards murmured that it was
getting dangerously light. This was true enough; the
sky was dimly blue. There was a tremendous noise of
excited voices coming from the Fascist redoubt. Evidently they had reoccupied the place in much greater
force than before. We were sixty or seventy yards from
the parapet when they must have seen or heard us, for
they sent over a heavy burst of fire which made us drop
on our faces. One of them flung a bomb over the parapet—a sure sign of panic. We were lying in the grass,

waiting for an opportunity to move on, when we either heard or thought we heard—I have no doubt it was pure imagination, but it seemed real enough at the time —that the Fascist voices were much closer. They had left the parapet and were coming after us. "Run!" I yelled to Moyle, and jumped to my feet. And heavens, how I ran! I had thought earlier in the night that you can't run when you are sodden from head to foot and weighted down with a rifle and cartridges; I learned now you can *always* run when you think you have fifty or a hundred armed men after you. But if I could run fast, others could run faster. In my flight something that might have been a shower of meteors sped past me. It was the three Spaniards, who had been in front. They were back to our own parapet before they stopped and I could catch up with them. The truth was that our nerves were all to pieces. I knew, however, that in a half light one man is invisible where five are clearly visible, so I went back alone. I managed to get to the outer wire and searched the ground as well as I could, which was not very well, for I had to lie on my belly. There was no sign of Jorge or Hiddlestone, so I crept back. We learned afterwards that both Jorge and Hiddlestone had been taken to the dressing-station earlier. Jorge was lightly wounded through the shoulder. Hiddlestone had received a dreadful wound—a bullet which travelled right up his left arm, breaking the bone in several places; as he lay helpless on the ground a bomb had burst near him and torn various other parts of his body. He recovered, I am glad to say. Later he told me that he had worked his way some distance lying on his back, then had clutched hold of a wounded Spaniard and they had helped one another in.

It was getting light now. Along the line for miles

around a ragged meaningless fire was thundering, like the rain that goes on raining after a storm. I remember the desolate look of everything, the morasses of mud, the weeping poplar trees, the yellow water in the trench-bottoms; and men's exhausted faces, unshaven, streaked with mud and blackened to the eyes with smoke. When I got back to my dug-out the three men I shared it with were already fast asleep. They had flung themselves down with all their equipment on and their muddy rifles clutched against them. Everything was sodden, inside the dug-out as well as outside. By long searching I managed to collect enough chips of dry wood to make a tiny fire. Then I smoked the cigar which I had been hoarding and which, surprisingly enough, had not got broken during the night.

Afterwards we learned that the action had been a success, as such things go. It was merely a raid to make the Fascists divert troops from the other side of Huesca, where the Anarchists were attacking again. I had judged that the Fascists had thrown a hundred or two hundred men into the counter-attack, but a deserter told us later on that it was six hundred. I dare say he was lying— deserters, for obvious reasons, often try to curry favour. It was a great pity about the telescope. The thought of losing that beautiful bit of loot worries me even now.

George Orwell initially went to Spain as a reporter but stayed to fight the Falangists with the POUM. This excerpt is from his highly acclaimed book Homage to Catalonia *(1952).*

KENNETH REXROTH

Requiem for the Spanish Dead

The great geometrical winter constellations
Lift up over the Sierra Nevada,
I walk under the stars, my feet on the known round
    earth.
My eyes following the lights of an airplane,
Red and green, growling deep into the Hyades.
The note of the engine rises, shrill, faint,
Finally inaudible, and the lights go out
In the southeast haze beneath the feet of Orion.

As the sound departs I am chilled and grow sick
With the thought that has come over me. I see Spain
Under the black windy sky, the snow stirring faintly,
Glittering and moving over the pallid upland,
And men waiting, clutched with cold and huddled
    together,
As an unknown planes goes over them. It flies southeast
Into the haze above the lines of the enemy,
Sparks appear near the horizon under it.

After they have gone out the earth quivers
And the sound comes faintly. The men relax for a
   moment
And grow tense again as their own thoughts return to
   them.

I see the unwritten books, the unrecorded experiments,
The unpainted pictures, the interrupted lives,
Lowered into the graves with the red flags over them.
I see the quick gray brains broken and clotted with
   blood,
Lowered each in its own darkness, useless in the earth.
Alone on a hilltop in San Francisco suddenly
I am caught in a nightmare, the dead flesh
Mounting over half the world presses against me.

Then quietly at first and then rich and full-bodied,
I hear the voice of a young woman singing.
The emigrants on the corner are holding
A wake for their oldest child, a driverless truck
Broke away on the steep hill and killed him,
Voice after voice adds itself to the singing.
Orion moves westward across the meridian,
Rigel, Bellatrix, Betelgeuse, marching in order,
The great nebula glimmering in his loins.

*Kenneth Rexroth's "Requiem for the Spanish Dead" first
appeared in a collection entitled* In What Hour *(1940).*

ARTHUR KOESTLER

Koestler's Own Story

I: MALAGA WAS IN DANGER

Twenty days after my arrest I received my first message
from the outside world. It was a ball of screwed brown
Spanish cigarette paper, flung through the spyhole of my
cell in the prison of Seville.

Unfolding it, I found a few lines scrawled in childish
handwriting with many spelling mistakes. It ran:

> 'Comrade:
>
> We know that you are here and that you are a
> friend of the Spanish Republic. You have been
> condemned to death: but they will not shoot you.
> They are too much afraid of the new King of
> England. They will only kill us—the poor and
> humble (*los pobres y humildes*).
>
> 'Yesterday again they shot seventeen in the ceme-
> tery. In our cell, where there were 100, there are
> only 73 now. Dear Comrade foreigner, we three are
> also condemned to death, and they will shoot us

this night or tomorrow. But you may survive and if you ever come out you must tell the world all about those who kill us because we want liberty and no Hitler.

'The victorious troops of our government have reconquered Toledo and we have also got Oviedo, Vitoria and Badajoz. And soon they will be here, and will carry us victoriously through the streets. Further letters will follow this one. Courage. We love you.

Three Republican Militiamen'

No further letters followed. As I learned later, two of these men were shot the same night and the third, whose sentence was commuted, was sent to the penitentiary for thirty years.

I never forgot that letter. I learned it by heart; every word is etched in my brain. It has literally become part of my body, for half an hour after I received it the inspection guard came into my cell. I had no time to tear up the paper and had to eat it.

I swore never to forget those *'pobres y humildes'*. I swore then and there that if ever I got out I would tell the world.

Since then I have been myself a prisoner for three months without news of the efforts that had been made by friends abroad to secure my release. Every time I was summoned from my cell I expected to be shot. Every time I lay down to sleep on my iron trestle, covered with a straw palliasse, I expected to die the next day.

Not until I reached Gibraltar from La Linea a week ago did I know for certain that I was safe. I find it still difficult to believe that I am in England, shaved and clean and—free.

But first I have to tell of the taking of Malaga where

I was captured and the long story of my imprisonment began.

In the middle of January the second division of the insurgent army, commanded by General Queipo de Llano and reinforced by approximately 50,000 Italian infantrymen, started the fatal offensive.

On the 25th the news became alarming. The rebels, we heard, had conquered Marbella on the Gibraltar road and Alhama on the Granada road—two strategic positions. It seemed that Malaga might fall any day.

On Tuesday, January 26, I left Valencia to find out what had happened and what was going to happen. I travelled by car, accompanied by a Norwegian journalist (Mrs Gerda Grepp), a Polish journalist (Mr Winter) and a chauffeur on the staff of the Spanish Ministry of Foreign Affairs.

We have passed through Alicante on the night of the 27th and reached Almeria in the south on the 28th. Here my diary of the last days of Malaga begins.

These notes, originally composed of about twenty typewritten pages, were confiscated when I was arrested in Malaga; but in the prison of Seville I was able to reconstruct them while the dates were still fresh in my memory and so smuggle out a second version hidden in my underclothing.

I leave unaltered these notes on the agony of a threatened city and of the strange behaviour of the people who lived and died in it. This although I realize that they contain some sharp, even bitter, criticism of the Republican authorities, who were partly responsible for the tragedy of Malaga.

But I swore on the memory of my three militiamen to

tell the whole truth, and I am keeping my promise. Perhaps, even, it may have a useful result.

Thursday, January 28, Almeria. Got up, still oppressed by talk yesterday with KST (a volunteer officer in the International Brigade) at Murcia. He said during the Italian tank attack at Prado front forty-two German Republican volunteers (some of them mutual friends) had been massacred in trench because they did not get order to retire in time. Useless and senseless hecatomb. Red tape and negligence everywhere.

10 a.m.—Saw British consul in Almeria, Campbell; following Spanish custom palavered, standing without being offered a seat. Nevertheless was nice and helpful. Says Malaga will be terrible butchery. City believed able to defend itself to last man; says all foreign consuls have left Malaga because of permanent air and sea bombardments. But British warships still in harbour—so still some hope of escape, if cut off.

Conversation cheered us up. These British consuls in forlorn Spanish cities are like pillars in the Apocalyptic flood: dry and solid.

At noon continued towards Malaga. Road becomes worse and worse. Flooded over at several points by streams of water coming down from the Sierras. Wonder how lorries with troops and ammunition can pass. As a matter of fact, they don't pass; the road, the only road, connecting Malaga with Republican Spain is absolutely deserted. Is Malaga already abandoned? Yet, we do not meet refugees either. It's ghostly.

Motril, 3 p.m.—Dirty little fisher-town. No one knows where headquarters are. Finally we find them in the municipal school.

Fresh search for military commander. At 4 p.m. we find him—an exhausted-looking youth with a five-days' beard, a former postmaster and member of Prieto's right-wing Socialist Party.

Shrugs shoulders in reply to our questions about absence of troops and arms supplies on road. Says, 'Three days ago twenty lorries arrived in Almeria with ammunition. They asked the local Syndicate to carry the load to Malaga because they had to go back.

'But Almeria Syndicate refused, claiming it needed its own cars for food supplies, and that the Valencia cars had to carry the load to Malaga. So the twenty lorries returned to Valencia and the munitions—badly needed —lingered somewhere in Almeria, and Malaga has no munitions. The Fascists may come in any time they like. Maybe you will meet them when you get there.'

Mrs Grepp is taking notes, only to tear them to pieces five minutes later. You can't cable such things, as a war correspondent.

'By the way,' says the Commander, 'you can't go on to Malaga. The bridge beyond Motril is broken. The road's flooded. You'll have to wait till the rain stops.'

'So Malaga is practically cut-off from the world?'

'As long as the rain lasts—yes.'

'And how long has it been raining now?'

'This is the fourth day, and then a week ago we had another wet period of ten days.'

'And how long has the bridge been broken?'

'Four or five months.'

'Then why, for God's sake, don't you repair it?'

Fresh shrugging of shoulders. 'We get no material or specialists from Valencia.'

The apathy of this man exasperates me.

'Don't you realize that Malaga is a strategic point—

perhaps the key to the war in the South, and that its fate depends on this bridge? I call this criminal negligence.'

The ex-postmaster gives me a long, untroubled look.

'You foreigners are always very nervous,' he says paternally.

'We may lose Malaga, and we may lose Madrid and half Catalonia, but we shall still win the war.'

There is a good deal of oriental fatalism in the Spanish manner of conducting the war on both sides: that is one reason why it drags on so long.

Other wars consist of succession of battles: this one of a succession of tragedies.

A little later we carry on despite the broken bridge. It costs us a detour of about 10 miles through practically impassable field paths, the last mile through a stream bed in 10 in. of water. Our light car gets through where a heavier vehicle would be bogged.

We arrive at Malaga about sunset. First impression:

A city after an earthquake. Darkness, entire streets in ruins; a pavement deserted, strewn with shells, and a certain odour which I knew from Madrid; fine chalk dust suspended in the air mixed with shell powder and —or is it imagination?—the penetrating smell of burnt flesh.

The straying lights of our headlamps glimmer on piles of debris and yet more debris. *Pulvis et nihil*— Madrid after the great bombardments was a health resort compared with this town in agony.

In the Regina Hotel unpleasant-looking but good-humoured militiamen are spitting on the marble pavement and eating the only available food—fried fish. We are the only guests of the hotel; the waiter tells us that this very afternoon a neighbouring house was destroyed by a 500-kilo bomb, killing fifty-two in this house alone.

The other waiters are gathered round the table discussing the bombardment and everyone's attitude during it: Bernardo hiding behind the table, Jesus looking out of the window and Dolores, the cook, crossing herself fifty-seven times before she fainted.

I take a stroll with Mrs Grepp. But the darkness is so menacing that we quickly return shivering and very uneasy. The porter looks at the sky full of stars and comments: 'Fine air raid weather tonight.' His daughter lost both her legs in the bombing of yesterday and he wonders whether the bridegroom will take her without legs.

Go to bed full of bad presentiments, trying to persuade myself that it is all fancy. I finish my notes, writing quite illogically in scribbled letters across my diary: 'Journey's end—*le voyage sans retour*.'

And so it proved for me and for many hundreds.

II: THE AGONY OF A CITY

No bread for breakfast, nothing but black coffee; the food supply of the town broken down by the same irresponsible negligence like the munition supply.

All the morning busy visiting offices: Propaganda Department and Civil Governor's house: meeting everywhere good will but hopeless red tape and disorganization.

After lunch, air-raid alarm; later, interview with Colonel Villalba, military commander of the Malaga forces. Admits frankly that things are going badly, but says, ten days ago, when he was appointed, they were still worse.

I inspected first the most exposed front: the coast road, Malaga–Marbella–Gibraltar. I found no trenches, no fortified positions, nothing but two militiamen in a mile's distance from the enemy's positions sitting on a milestone and smoking cigarettes. 'Where are your troops?' I asked them. 'Somewhere in the barracks,' they said. 'If the Fascists were to attack us we would see it and have plenty of time to warn them; why should they sit out in the rain?'

Visiting systematically the different sectors of the Malaga front: the roads to Marbella, Alfernate, Antequera. Everywhere the same impression; no second defence line, no arms, no munitions, a few improvised trenches or stone barricades, absolutely useless against a possible tank attack.

Last night, after a relatively quiet week, Queipo de Llano started his final offensive against Malaga.

The attack began, very surprisingly, in the sector Ardales–El Burgo; and—still more surprising—it was hit back. Watched the fighting from a hill. Awful butchery. Spoke to a deserter, Antonio Pedro Jimenez, from Dos Hermanos, near Seville. Says, in Dos Hermanos there is a newly established munition factory, built and run by Italians; says, all through the night ten to twenty lorries are carrying Italian infantry to Malaga front.

Late afternoon visited headquarters, asked Commander Alfredo G. how things are going on. Says: '*Ça va mal,'* enemy attacking simultaneously all sectors. Asked how long he thinks the town may resist. Says three days maximum. Can't get any message through censorship.

Rebel cruisers *Canarias, Baleares, Almirante Cervera,* and three smaller rebel warships bombarding all day over the coast north and south of Malaga. Where is the Republican fleet? Invisible. The rebels are uncontested masters of sea and air. No food, no munitions. First symptoms of panic in the town. Learn that Civil Governor L. A. deserted to Valencia. Last wire-line destroyed near Motril. Try to get through by Marconi cable via Gibraltar, but don't know whether my messages arrive in London.

At night Commander Alfredo comes to have dinner with me at the hotel. Says Alfernate and Ventas de Zefareya lost: that means the end. Mrs Grepp (Polish journalist) says she will leave tomorrow. Then I shall be the last Mohican of the world Press.

Several air raids during the morning. Without news from London since Thursday, so feel sure my messages don't get through. Went to Civil Governor's office, trying to find out whether I could use radio for SOS message telling the world that Italian troops are going to capture Malaga. But at the Governor's office everybody lost his head. Went to headquarters with same intention, but Villalba is invisible and has left order that *'la Presse'* —*la Presse, c'est moi!*—is not allowed to cable anything about the military situation except optimistic propaganda stuff. Army people always believe that if they call a defeat a victory it is a victory and the dead will stand up. They believe in the magic effects of propaganda lies like bushmen in the prayers of the witch-doctor.

In the meantime, Mrs Grepp got ready to leave. An official takes her in his car to Valencia. I have just time to scribble a few words on a piece of paper, which she should phone from Valencia to London, to the Foreign Editor of the *News Chronicle*: 'Malaga lost. K staying.'

At 2 p.m. the exodus from Malaga begins. The road to Valencia is a flooding stream of lorries, cars, mules, carriages, frightened, quarrelling people.

Impossible to know what is going on the fronts. At 4 p.m. I leave in my car for Velez. The sight is simply frightful. The militiamen of the routed army—bearded, exhausted, starving—linger in the cafés, in doorways, public buildings, lie sleeping on the pavements. There is no order, no more command, complete chaos.

As soon as we get back to Malaga, stopping at headquarters, my chauffeur, who has got the contagion of the panic, declares categorically that he won't stay any longer. As a matter of fact, I have neither the right nor the power to hold him back; I only ask him to take my luggage from the hotel to Sir Peter Chalmers Mitchell's house, as Sir Peter has invited me to stay with him if the situation becomes critical. Ten minutes later chauffeur and car disappear on the Valencia road, with them the last possibility of getting away.

It is dawn now. I feel very lonely, abandoned, and sit down on the staircase of headquarters. Commander Alfredo comes along and sits down beside me. After a while he says: 'This is probably our last night. The road will be cut off in a few hours, and they will kill us like rats in a trap.'

'What are you going to do if they come in?'

He taps his revolver. 'I have still got five cartridges. Four for the Fascists, the fifth for myself.'

I have the uneasy feeling that he is acting as in a show, and the absurd idea comes to me that Alfredo and all the others, including myself, are children, playing Walter Scott heroes and unable to imagine the reality of death.

It is completely dark now; and the uninterrupted grumbling of cannons and coughing of machine guns behind the hill.

Alfredo takes me to the officers' casino. I fill my pockets with dry bread and two bottles of cognac. Then I stagger through the dead-dark city to Sir Peter's house, with the Union Jack planted on the white roof.

(I had paid my first visit to Sir Peter two days after my arrival in Malaga. He was, after the Consul's departure, the only Englishman in Malaga.

'I am going to stay,' he told me, 'when the rebels come in. If they know that I am here—a foreign observer—it may have some attenuating effect and even prevent a second Badajoz. And, besides, if they don't shoot me, I wish to give evidence afterwards to the world on the Malaga tragedy.'

I told Sir Peter that I had come with the same intention, and he invited me to stay in his house.)

Breakfast air raid at 8 a.m. The noise of artillery and machine guns doesn't stop any more. Later on, another air raid. Lola, Sir Peter's housemaid, suffers an hysterical attack.

After lunch—lunch is an exaggeration—went down

to town. Since yesterday the physiognomy of the town completely changed; no more tramways, all shops closed, groups at every corner and all faces covered with the grey spider's-web of fear. Just while passing Caleta Bridge a squadron of six rebel planes pass very low above our heads, sowing murder. I look for shelter beyond the bridge; there are two militiamen drinking cognac, one singing the 'Internationale', the other, in low voice and with a stupid smile, the hymn of the Falange (the Spanish Fascists). I feel how the contagion of fear gets me, too.

Get in to headquarters; it looks like a night asylum; sleeping, unhuman-looking men on the desks and floors. While waiting to be received by Colonel Villalba, an exhausted sergeant staggers in and is conducted immediately to the chief commander. I enter with him.

'What news?' asks Villalba.

'They are coming with fifteen tanks down the Colmenar road.'

'How far are they?'

'An hour ago they were five miles from the city.'

'Resistance?'

'None. Our people threw away their rifles and dispersed in the Sierra.'

'Thank you.'

The sergeant puts himself below a table and falls immediately asleep. Villalba has a short, whispered conversation with some of his staff officers. An order is issued to an adjutant and they leave the room rather hurriedly.

I stopped Villalba. 'What do you want?' he says nervously. 'You see that I am in a hurry. I can give you the following statement: The situation is difficult, but Malaga will defend itself.'

'Where are you going?' I ask him. But he is already out.

I rush to a window and look down. Villalba and his staff officers get into a car. Everybody is looking rather embarrassed. The car leaves the courtyard.

'Where did he go?' I ask an officer whom I know.

'He deserted,' the officer says, calmly.

'It was his duty to leave,' says another one. 'We will be cut off in an hour, and he is the commander of the entire southern sector: so he had to leave.'

'How can he command if we are cut off?'

'He deserted,' repeats the first.

'Who is the chief now?' I ask.

'The chief?' Everybody looks surprised. Nobody knows.

I passed to another room. There is Commander Alfredo sitting behind a typewriter. It is all like a bad dream. I note, that he is using the red half of the ribbon. I read:

'To whom it may concern. This is to certify that Commander Alfredo G. is leaving on an important mission to Valencia. Authorities are requested to let him pass.'

'You too, Alfredo?' I ask him.

He blushes. 'And you, too. I take you in my car. It is all over.'

That is no more Walter Scott. It is rather James Joyce.

In the courtyard we find X, a mutual friend. He is ill, high fever, coughing and spitting.

'Come,' says Alfredo, 'it is all over.'

'Go to hell. I stay,' says X.

'Villalba left too. We take you by force,' says Alfredo, tears in his eyes.

'Go to hell,' says X. (He is dead now. Eighty per cent of the persons mentioned in this story are dead.)

We step into Alfredo's car. Alfredo's mother is in the car and Alfredo's sister and some other women, and all are crying and sobbing.

When the car starts I remember Sir Peter; during the last hour I have completely forgotten him.

'We must take my English friend,' I say to Alfredo.

'Impossible,' says the chauffeur. 'The Fascists are on the New Road; his house is cut off.'

'But I left him an hour ago!'

'They came in since. Don't you hear the machine guns?'

I am hesitating. We reach the city barrier. The crowd of refugees stares at us, privileged owners of a car, with envy and hatred.

I have a sudden attack of deep disgust and something like a nervous breakdown.

'Stop,' I say to the chauffeur, 'I want to go back.'

'Don't stop,' says Alfredo.

I jump out of the car. Alfredo gesticulates. The car disappears in the crowd.

It is dawn again. I walk slowly to Sir Peter's house. The Fascists are not yet in.

They came in only the next day.

III: AT THE MERCY OF FRANCO

Since my return to London I have received several letters and personal visits from relatives of British people who are detained for political reasons in Franco's prisons.

They have all asked me not to publish anything that may annoy the rebel authorities, fearing that those unfortunates who are at the mercy of the rebels, would have to pay for it.

Now, as a matter of fact, my liberation was not due to an act of grace on the part of Franco, but was the consequence of an exchange—a simple business transaction, with human lives as the merchandise.

I have, therefore, no reason to be thankful to Franco, nor any moral obligation towards him, not to tell the truth about how they treated me and my fellow-prisoners.

It seems, further, rather unlikely that an objective exposure of facts could influence the fate of other prisoners; first, because both sides are equally interested in effecting exchanges—until now about 2,000 prisoners have been exchanged by the intermediary action of the British authorities—and, secondly, because any reprisals against prisoners on one side would induce similar measures on the other side. Their fate is mutually bound by a tragic chain.

Nevertheless, being aware of the grave responsibility which the above-mentioned circumstances induce, I feel obliged to satisfy the demands of mothers and wives who are still suffering the same hell of anxiety and dread which my wife suffered until a few days ago.

With the agreement of the editor of the *News Chronicle*, I have decided, therefore, to delete from my articles anything that may 'annoy the rebels'—a task not easy to accomplish.

I shall say nothing about the details of my arrest, about how my fellow-prisoners and I were treated in the prisons of Malaga, Seville, and La Linea. Being at last physically free, I have had to learn that liberty is a very relative thing.

But I feel sure that the hour when this nightmare of a war will end and when I regain my entire liberty is not very far off now—and I have the firm hope that it will end in such a way that the Spanish Republic will also regain its liberty.

I told you in my last article how those who were responsible for the defence of Republican Malaga deserted the helpless city on Sunday, February 7, 1937.

Since then the Valencia Government—as a message announced only yesterday—has decided that the men responsible for the fall of Malaga will be tried and punished.

Following are extracts from my diary of the day when the rebel troops entered Malaga, and I was staying in the house of Sir Peter Chalmers Mitchell.

Monday, February 8

8 a.m. During breakfast observed through glasses, rebel cruisers, flying the yellow-red-yellow Bourbon flag, entering the port of Malaga. Waiting for the beginning of the bombardment; but they don't shoot.

8:30 a.m. Rebel aeroplanes revolving over us in the sky. But they don't drop bombs.

9 a.m. Usual hour for beginning of the artillery bombardment. But not a single detonation. Sunshine and dead, ghostly silence.

10 a.m. A wounded militiaman, unarmed, trembling, and half-dead, passes before the house, asking for water and cigarettes. While I give him a light, his arms and feet are trembling.

'Is the road to the town still free?' he asks.

'Yes—still free.'

'They will not kill me?'

'They will not kill you.'

'Are you sure that they will not kill me?'

'I am sure that they will not kill you.'

'God bless you, señor.'

And he staggers on. (I wonder whether they did kill him.)

11 a.m. Rebel cruisers and planes continue their peaceful promenade in the waters and airs of still Republican Malaga.

Sir Peter and I decide to go to town, to find out what is happening.

Immediately after we leave the house an invisible machine gun in the neighbourhood starts barking; the road is under fire. We run back; a refugee family enters the garden. We greet them, as we are accustomed, by raising the fist—the usual greeting in Republican Spain—but they don't move their hands. We ask them where the rebels are, and the woman says, whispering. 'The Nationalists are everywhere, in the hills—here, there. Since morning there has been a white flag on the tower of the Civil Governor's.'

So it is over. Malaga has surrendered.

And I remember Colonel Villalba's last statement before he stepped into his car: 'The situation is difficult, but Malaga will resist.'

I have a water-glass full of cognac.

1 p.m. An officer, wearing the grey steel-helmet of the Italian Army, appears on the road leading to Colmenar just opposite our house.

He looks around and fires a revolver-shot to the air.

Immediately after about 200 infantrymen in perfect order come down the road. They sing Mussolini's hymn, the '*Giovinezza*'.

Passing before the house they salute us, and the house-people, yesterday still diligently raising their fists, now raise their arms in the Roman Fascist greeting with the same Spanish effusiveness. They seem perfectly at their ease, but, as they consider us foreigners as half imbeciles, the gardener warns Sir Peter and me to change our attitude too, 'because we have a new Government now'. It is tragic-comic and humiliating.

After a certain time, as more and more troops pass and greet us—we are all gathered on the balcony as if we were reviewing a military parade—after a certain time Sir Peter and I have to raise our arms too. We avoid looking at one another.

3 p.m. A company of Italian infantry occupies the neighbouring hill.

4 p.m. A clamour of hurrahs and clapping comes from the town. The rebels have entered Malaga.

4:30 p.m. Cars with the Bourbon flag circulate over the roads. Tanks are coming down from Colmenar. The detonation of shots comes in regular intervals from the town. Someone among the house-people puts forward the suggestion that, as the fighting is over, these shots may mean 'the beginning of the executions of the Red criminals . . .'

I am burning some compromising papers. Introduction-letters of the Spanish Embassy and of well-known politicians in Valencia.

It is definitely over. We are at the mercy of Queipo de Llano. Unhappily, I know him from before.

. . .

Tuesday, February 9. Arrested at 11 a.m.
The history of the arrest of Sir Peter Chalmers Mitchell and of myself is attached to a chain of extraordinary co-incidences, which confirms the old proverb that life is the best novel-author.

I have to go back to the past. In August, 1936, one month after the civil war started, I visited, as a special correspondent of the *News Chronicle*, Lisbon and Seville and was received by General Queipo de Llano.

Like all journalists, I had to keep in close contact with Captain B, head of the Press Department of the Burgos Government. In consequence of an argument with a Nazi correspondent and some German war-pilots in the hall of the Hotel Cristina in Seville, I was de-nounced to Captain B as a notorious and incorrigible Left Wing Liberal and preferred, therefore, to leave for Gibraltar, rather precipitately.

Never again was a Liberal correspondent allowed to enter rebel territory; and Captain B swore, as I was told later by a French colleague, 'whenever he gets hold of K to shoot him on the spot'.

It was precisely Captain B who got hold of me in Malaga.

Now, Captain B happened to have a cousin living in Malaga; and this cousin—let us call him Señor B—happened to owe his life to Sir Peter, who saved him from the Anarchists.

Señor B owned the garden and the house neighbour-ing Sir Peter's garden and house. Señor B was a member of the Fascist 'Falange', and when the Fascist revolt was crushed in Malaga in July, 1936, he came to Sir Peter's house, asking for protection and shelter.

Sir Peter installed Señor B on the upper floor of his

house, in the same room which I afterwards occupied, and Señor B handed him over his documents in an envelope, which Sir Peter locked in his writing desk.

Next day an Anarchist patrol came to the house.

They did not want to trouble Sir Peter, knowing his sympathetic attitude towards the Republican government; but they wanted to see the documents of the Señor living upstairs.

Sir Peter had to hand over the documents. The Anarchist chief, a young boy, opened the envelope. The first thing he found was a membership-card of the 'Falange'; the second, an illustrated programme of a Paris music-hall. He seemed very pleased with both discoveries.

Sir Peter had one of his usual happy inspirations.

'Look here,' he said in his softest voice, 'we'll make an exchange: you keep the programme and I'll keep the card.'

The Anarchist who, as I have said, was very young, was first indignant, then amused, and finally, out of sympathy with Sir Peter, he agreed.

Some days later Señor B, with the help of Sir Peter and of the British Consul in Malaga, escaped to Gibraltar.

His luggage remained in Sir Peter's house, his house was transformed into a military hospital.

Señor B returned the day after the rebels conquered Malaga and dropped in to Sir Peter's house to fetch his luggage, on Tuesday, February 9, at 11 a.m., at the very moment when his cousin, accompanied by two other officers, arrested me, his revolver pointed on my neck.

So I was saved—for the moment at least—by an old programme of a Paris music-hall.

If this story had happened in a film it would have been a bad film.

IV: INSIDE A REBEL PRISON

As I told you, I was arrested on Tuesday, February 9, at 11 a.m. by Captain B from the Burgos Press Department. While my hands were being tied, and, following the custom on such solemn occasions, the revolvers of Captain B and two other officers were pointed at me, Sir Peter Chalmers Mitchell entered the room.

I was convinced that Captain B was going to shoot me on the spot. Sir Peter was very pale, and I thought he might collapse—he is a man of seventy-three.

Again I had the feeling that it was all a bad dream and that it didn't concern *me* at all. It was a kind of merciful psychic narcosis, which Nature always provides in critical moments. I heard myself saying, to my own astonishment: 'Look here, B, if you are going to shoot me, take me upstairs; don't do it in Sir Peter's presence.'

Afterwards I often wondered—I had all the time in prison to deal with such problems—whether these words, which maybe saved my life, were induced by consideration for Sir Peter or just by the motive to gain time. Maybe it was a mixture of both; but I think the second predominated.

In the meantime Sir Peter was arrested, too, but his hands were not tied.

Then Señor B, Captain B's cousin, dropped in to fetch his luggage. Although Señor B, a member of the Fascist Falange, owed his life to Sir Peter, who had saved him from the Anarchists (as I related yesterday), he seemed

rather pleased at the scene which he found in his bene-
factor's house.

The two Bs and Sir Peter had a short conversation in
the next room. Sir Peter obviously was pleading for me,
but just as obviously without much success.

I was not allowed to approach them. 'What is going
on?' I shouted through the open door. They came out,
and Sir Peter said, very quietly and with a tender look,
'It seems all right for me but not for you.'

Anyhow, they did not shoot me on the spot.

They took us to a car. When we passed the Italian
troops beyond the hill they seemed not unwilling to
lynch us; but Captain B persuaded them that it wouldn't
be nice to do that.

We were taken to the police station. Captain B went
out and we had to wait in the car with the two other
officers.

We waited two hours. The sun shone: it was very
hot. I don't remember what we talked about, and I
suppose most of it was nonsense; everything is nonsense
when facing the imminent reality of being shot. But I
remember Sir Peter reciting to me these verses of Swin-
burne which he knew I liked very much and which
appear on the front page of his recently published
memoirs.

> *Pray thou thy days be long before*
>   *thy death,*
> *And full of ease and kingdom:*
>   *seeing in death*
> *There is no comfort and none*
>   *aftergrowth,*
> *Nor shall one thence look up and*
>   *see day's dawn*

> *Nor light upon the land whither I*
>   *go*
> *Live thou and take thy fill of days*
>   *and die*
> *When thy day comes; and make*
>   *not much of death*
> *Lest ere thy day thou reap an evil*
>   *thing.*

Then we separated.

They took me into the police station. There I had to wait for another two hours. I don't want to speak about what I saw and heard there, for the reasons which I mentioned yesterday.

Some time in the afternoon—I had lost all sense of time—Captain B came back and gave orders to search me thoroughly.

To be searched was just the thing which I feared more than to be tortured or beaten. I had a treasure in my pocket, the most useful thing in the circumstances: a morphine syringe with a reserve needle and a quantity of morphinae hydrochloridum; sufficient to get anyone out of all troubles of the Spanish Civil War.

Sir Peter had obtained two such syringes from a medical mission in case anyone of his household should be wounded in an air bombardment and no medical help was available.

In the last critical days he had handed me over one of the syringes, as we both disliked the idea of being captured alive. All this may appear somewhat romantic and exalted; but in abnormal situations human reactions are abnormal, too, and a civil war is just the most abnormal and mad thing which human fantasy can imagine.

Now they searched me. While waiting in the police station I had managed to hide the syringe among my cigarettes and to push the needle in the lining of my jacket hoping to be able to make use of it in an unobserved moment.

But the soldier who searched me, drawing his hand along my jacket, suddenly pricked himself with the needle.

'What's that?' he asked. I showed him the needle and he and his companions all retreated panic stricken, thinking it was some murderous poisoned instrument—Spaniards like reading detective stories just as we do.

In all despair I had some little satisfaction in seeing these warriors childishly frightened, and I couldn't help appreciating the insane humour of the situation. '*Galgenhumor*' the Germans call that—the laughter under the gibbet.

They emptied my pockets and confiscated everything. I still had some Catalan money, which has no value in rebel territory. 'This you may keep,' one of the soldiers told me rather good-humouredly. 'You may pay your ticket with it when you undertake your journey to heaven tonight.'

I asked them to leave me my fountain pen.

'You won't need it in heaven,' they said.

They put me into a lorry; five soldiers, their rifles in their hands, took their places behind me.

It was already dark; and once again I was convinced that the moment had come when they were going to shoot me.

I am afraid that I repeat myself, but the fault is in the facts: for three months every new situation, every opening of my cell, gave me the same impression that the supreme moment had come. It seems monotonous, but I can assure you it wasn't for me.

I asked one of the soldiers where they were going to take me. He said they were going to take me to prison. It was an immense relief and at the same time a disappointment: I thought the sooner it would be over the better.

The soldiers handed me over to the prison authorities, together with a letter in which it was stated that I was a very dangerous person—I suppose that was the effect of the needle—that I should be thoroughly watched and kept 'incomunicado'—that is to say, isolated: and that I was a 'cosa internacional'—an 'international case'.

I stayed for three days in a cell of the Malaga prison. Being a 'cosa internacional' I was treated correctly, being neither beaten nor held in chains. Of the general conditions in the prison I shall not speak.

After three days—on Saturday, February 13—the cell door opened and two civil guards took me out. We went in a car to the railway station and took the train—the first regular train from Malaga to Seville.

We travelled in an overcrowded third-class compartment. The passengers—Andalusian peasants—behaved extremely nicely to me; they gave me sausage and cigarettes and Andalusian sweets. They tried to cheer me up. 'Eat, eat, poor devil,' they said to me, 'as long as you are still alive, eat sausage and cheese—afterwards it's too late.'

I shivered: one of them gave me his coat. It was almost a political demonstration.

The two civil guards after a time also melted a little: they untied my hands and shared their cigarettes and food with me. They showed me the letter which accompanied me, and I learned that I was being transferred to Seville to be put 'at the disposal of the chief of the armed forces of the Southern district—General Queipo de Llano.'

I knew General Queipo from before, as I knew Captain B—from my first visit to Seville in August, 1936. Unfortunately I had reasons to believe that it wouldn't be a mutual pleasure to meet again.

We arrived in Seville at night. The two civil guards took me to the prison where I was to live for the next three months and took leave of me like old friends with a nice handshake. The prison officials looked rather astonished.

For the first six days nothing happened. I walked up and down in my cell, and the arrival of my food at regular intervals was the only event of my days.

On Friday, February 19, the iron door of the cell swung open and three officers of the Falange stepped in. Two of them were men; the third was a young woman.

They greeted me very politely and I apologized for being unable to offer the young uniformed lady a better seat than the straw mattress of my bed. But she smiled—a rather charming smile as it seemed—and asked whether I was Mr Koestler, whether I spoke English. I replied in the affirmative to both questions. Then she asked me if I was a Communist. I had to reply in the negative to this.

'But you are a Red, aren't you?'

I said that I was in sympathy with the Valencia Government but didn't belong to any party.

The young lady asked whether I was aware what consequences my activity would have. I said I wasn't.

'Well,' she said, 'it means death.'

I asked why.

She said because I was supposed to be a spy.

I said that I wasn't, and that I had never heard of a spy who signed with his own name articles against one party in a war and afterwards went to the territory of that party with his passport in his pocket.

She said the authorities would investigate that point, but that in the meantime General Franco had been asked to spare my life by the *News Chronicle* and by Mr H in New York; that she was the correspondent of the newspapers of Mr H in Spain; and that General Franco had said he might reprieve me.

For me this was rather astonishing news.

V: DIALOGUE WITH DEATH

So the tenth day of my imprisonment—Friday, February 19—I learn that I am condemned to death and that maybe Franco will grant commutation—that means, according to Spanish law, thirty years in prison.

The young lady who brought me this news, and who happened to be the correspondent of a chain of American newspapers, asked me whether I wanted to make a statement for her newspapers on my feelings towards General Franco.

Now, if you note that word 'maybe' in the first sentence of this article you will easily understand the logical implications of the young lady's question. It was something like a Biblical temptation, although Satan presented himself in the smiling mask of a young girl journalist; and at that moment—after the infernal days of waiting for torture and death—I had not the moral force to resist.

So I said that although I did not know Franco personally I had the feeling that he must be a man of humanitarian ideas whom I might entirely trust. The young lady wrote this down, seemed very pleased and asked me to sign it.

I took the pen, and then I realized I was going to sign my own moral death sentence; and that this sentence nobody could commute. So I crossed out what I had written and dictated another statement, which ran:

> I don't know General Franco personally, and he doesn't know me; so if he grants me commutation I must suppose that it would be mainly a political act.
>
> Nevertheless, I could not help being personally thankful to him, as a man thanks another who has saved his life. But I believe in the Socialist conception of the human future, and shall never cease to believe in it.

This statement I signed.

There was no need to tell you about the previous moment of weakness. But I don't pretend to play a heroic role and prefer the human one.

The day after the visit I felt an immense relief. The second day I remembered the fatal 'maybe'; the third day it became an obsession.

Uncertainty is half of death, says Cervantes; and so it is. Everybody has his own philosophy of death. As for me, I am not afraid of death, but very afraid of the act of dying. During three months I remembered at least ten times a day the verse of Rilke:

'Lord, I do not ask Thee for a worthy life, but grant me the favour of a worthy death.'

Now, to be executed in a civil war is just one of the unpleasant manners of dying. And I had all the time to think it over and over. You think a tremendous lot if you are alone and have got nothing to do but to walk up and down and up and down, six and a half steps up and six and a half steps down, for at least eighteen hours a day; and that during ninety-seven days.

It was frightful, but not so frightful as the reader may imagine it. Human nature disposes of astonishing mental resources of which you do not know in normal circumstances. It is just a question of inner discipline and mental exercise to mobilize these forces and to obtain with their help a state of mind which enables you to regard your personal fate as unimportant, and life and death with relative indifference.

But, of course, you cannot live permanently on the top of a magic mountain, and there were hours, even entire days, of an almost absolute despair impossible to describe. But there were also events of great joy, of an almost absolute happiness, which I had never known since I was a child and maybe never shall know again.

Such events were: when I got a piece of soap and a comb (ninth day); two cigarettes (thirteenth day); a pencil and five sheets of paper (twenty-seventh day); five new sheets of paper (thirty-third day); the first book— John Stuart Mill's autobiography in a Spanish translation (thirty-fifth day); and so on.

One of the best achievements of the young Spanish Republic are the so-called 'model prisons', of Madrid, Barcelona, Seville. They are built on the most advanced principles and are the best in Europe. The cell windows are spacious and look on the big *'patio'* (courtyard). Every cell is furnished with an iron bed, a straw mattress; an iron table and chair; a wash-basin with flowing cold water, and a w.c.

Of course, the present abnormal conditions affect prison life too. The Seville prison is overcrowded; with a normal capacity of 800 it has 1,300 prisoners, and most of the single cells are occupied by four or even five prisoners.

The warders and lower ranks of the prison staff are still the men of the 'ancient regime'; that means that they still have some of the humanitarian traditions of the Republic. About 50 per cent of the warders belong now to the Falange (the Spanish Fascist Party), but with a few exceptions their attitude towards the prisoners, and especially towards the political prisoners, has not changed. They are indifferent, or kind; some of them even very kind and nice. As I said, I am speaking only of the lower staff. During my sojourn in the prison of Seville none of the prisoners was beaten or physically ill-treated.

The food was the regular prison food—rather bad coffee in the morning, soup at noon and more soup at night with sufficient white bread. After a certain time I became almost accustomed to it.

At 6.45 a.m. a trumpet sounded the hour to get up. At 7.30 the prisoners, except those who were kept isolated like me, were let out on the *patio,* where, according to the Spanish prison custom, they passed practically the whole day.

There are two *patios,* a smaller one with trees and flowers, almost a garden, originally designed for the political prisoners, and a bigger one, without trees and without flowers, for the criminals. But since the civil war began the roles have changed: now the political prisoners are in the 'bad *patio*' and the murderers, thieves and robbers enjoy the flowers in the garden.

At 8.30, breakfast; at 12.30, the first soup. At one o'clock the prisoners are taken from the *patio* back to their cells, where they pass the siesta hours until 3 p.m.

From 3 till 7 they promenade again in the *patio*; at 7 the night soup; at 9.30 the trumpet again, and to bed.

Yes, the day-life in prison is quite normal. But there are the nights.

Those who are condemned to death are shot between midnight and two in the morning.

I have a feeling of sickness remembering the night when I first heard these executions.

I woke up about midnight. In the silence of the prison, the black air charged with the nightmare dreams of 1,300 sleeping men, I heard the murmured prayer of the priest and the ringing of the mass bell.

Then a cell door, the third to the left of mine, was opened and a name was called. A sleepy voice asked '*Que?*' ('What?'), and the priest's voice immediately became stronger and the bell rang louder.

And now the sleepy man in his cell understood. At the beginning he only moaned, then with a suffocated voice he asked for help: '*Socorro! socorro!*'

'Man, there is no help,' said the warder accompanying the priest.

He said it neither in a hostile nor a friendly manner, just as stating a fact. For a moment the man who was going to die kept silent; the sober, quiet voice of the warder puzzled him. And then he began to laugh.

It was not the loud, shrill laughter of actors who play a man becoming mad; the man tapped his knees with his hands and his laughter was rather quiet and oppressed, gulping and hiccoughing. 'You are making fun,' he said to the priest. 'I knew at once that you were making fun.'

'Man, this is no fun,' said the warder in the same dry voice as before.

Then they took him out through the main entrance of the prison. I heard him shouting outside. But the detonation came only a few minutes later.

In the meantime the priest and the warder had opened the next cell, the second on my left. (We, the condemned to death, occupied a series of neighbouring cells.)

Again: '*Que?*' And again the prayer and the bell. This one was weeping and sobbed through his nose like a child. Then he asked for his mother: '*Madre; madre!*'

The warder said, 'Man, why did you not think about her before?'

They took him out.

They went to the next door. When my neighbour was called he did not say anything. Most probably he was already awake like me, and prepared. But when the priest ended his prayer he asked, as if of himself: 'Why must I die?' The priest answered with five words, pronounced with a solemn voice, but rather in a hurry: 'Faith, man. Death means liberty.'

They took him out.

They came to my cell, and the priest pushed the bolt back. I saw him through the spy-hole.

'No, not this one,' said the warder.

They went to the next door. He was prepared, too. He did not ask questions. While the priest prayed, he began in a low voice to sing the 'Marseillaise'. But after a few bars his voice broke and he, too, sobbed.

They took him out . . .

Until April 14—exactly two months after my transfer to Seville—I was hermetically isolated from the outside world and was not allowed to get out of my cell.

On April 14 I was allowed for the first time to exercise for two hours in the courtyard. When I came out to the fresh air I collapsed.

It was at 1 p.m., during the siesta hours, when the 'normal', non-isolated prisoners were in their cells. But there were three others out in the courtyard with me; all three condemned to death, too.

One of them was Nicolas, a former militiaman. He gave me a piece of green salad which he had got from his wife.

The second day, when I came out at one o'clock we were only three. Nicolas had been shot the previous night.

The same day—April 14—I was allowed for the first time to write a letter. I wrote to the British Consul at Seville, and a second time, three days later. On the 21st I received the Consul's reply, telling me that he had asked the authorities for permission to see me.

On the 28th I received the Consul's first visit and heard for the first time that the British Government and British public opinion took a friendly interest in my case.

On May 4 I got a companion in my cell. He was an Italian officer of Franco's army, arrested because of some insignificant dispute with the Spanish civil guards.

On the previous night he had heard executions and had an hysterical attack: both his legs became temporarily paralysed.

He told me that he was with the Italian troops who

who conquered Malaga—now I had to nurse him. To the astonishment of both of us we became good friends.

On May 8 the Military Judge of investigation came, and for the first time since my arrest I was interrogated.

I asked the judge what the charge against me was. He said, that according to military law, the charge was kept secret. But I happened to see the cover of my dossier and learned that the accusation was 'aiding military rebellion'.

So the charge of spying was dropped by the rebel authorities themselves. Nevertheless, 'aiding military rebellion' is a charge which involves capital punishment.

Four days later—it was Coronation Day, but I didn't know it—my cell door opened and I was taken out of prison. I had no idea where we were going or what would happen.

They took me to the aviation camp; there a little baby Douglas machine was waiting. It had only two seats—one for the pilot, one for me.

An hour later we landed at La Linea, the Spanish frontier station next to Gibraltar.

There I learned that I would be exchanged for a prisoner of the Valencia Government—Señora Hayja, wife of the pilot who had brought me there.

I could not believe it. I was absolutely dazed. It was all like a dream.

I had to wait two days in La Linea prison. But at last, on Friday, May 14, I stepped through the iron gate which separates the land of war from the land of peace —the entry to the blessed soil of Gibraltar.

It is still like a dream . . .

Arthur Koestler went to Spain as a journalist (a cover for his Comintern activities). He was imprisoned in Seville for several months under sentence of death. After his release, he filed "Koestler's Own Story" for the News Chronicle *(May 1937).*

WYNDHAM LEWIS

The Revenge for Love

It was a day of suffocating heat. Squadrons of mosquitoes, in close formation, manœuvred in the air of the ward, and advanced, in a hysterical drone, to the attack. The Briton and the Basque ate their lunch beneath their mosquito-curtains; they conversed with each other like a couple of heavily-veiled brides, peering at each other's shadowy head short-sightedly through the vestal netting.

A groaner had got into the neighbouring ward. Since the evening before he had been heard there. His groans were the deepest and grimmest either of them had believed possible—and both knew what a groan was when they saw it. Percy had been wounded in the War, and had served his apprenticeship in that pandemonium orchestra. As to the Basque, he came from a country of keeners and groaners, and as a stripling had been a keen groaner himself.

'I once heard a snorer who was nearly as bad as that,' said Percy. 'But I've never heard a groaner who could touch him!'

'Nor I, Percilito!'

'Ah well! I suppose it pleases Sister Teresa! She must really feel she's in Dante's inferno. So it probably makes somebody happy!'

'I don't believe it could make anybody happy.'

'I believe you're wrong. Teresa has looked ten years younger this morning. She's a new woman since he's been here.'

Altogether it had been a bad day up to date. And after their lunch they started an argument about *classes*. It was a hot day for this subject. But where the Marxian *class* counter was in question—and who brought it up neither quite knew, they seemed to have done so to-gether—neither Virgilio nor Percy would allow himself to be daunted by a spot of heat.

'The vertical classes of Capitalism,' Percy had strongly contended, 'are better than the horizontal classes of Fascism.'

'Better still *no* classes! *No* classes are better still,' Virgilio had replied hotly and mournfully.

'*Claro!* That is self-evident.' Percy was by this time a little cross. He found it difficult to digest his food in the horizontal position, and he had to get a little cross in order to shake it down. It had started to go down quite nicely. A belch or two had announced its downward drift. 'But class, Virgilito, of *some* sort there always *must* be.'

Virgilio squinted at him suspiciously through his white bridal veil—as one bride might at another who had been guilty of too flippant an observation.

'No, señor!' he said a little violently. 'If you permit *that* much class'—and he measured off a fraction of a class no longer than a half of his fingernail, the dirty half—'you let in *all* classes!'

'Give Class an inch and it will take an ell!' said Percy pleasantly.

'That is so.'

'I agree with you. In principle, Class must be banished from the new communist society. But you cannot in practice abolish class. Stalin and his great commissars after all constitute *a class*. An administrative caste. We know that.'

'But they are not hereditary.'

'We cannot even say that. They are not supposed to be. A century hence that would be easier to answer.'

'I don't understand you.'

'You never do. What I am saying is only common sense. Class, in some form, *must* persist.'

There was a restless movement from under Virgilio's mosquito curtain.

'And it is better,' Percy concluded, with rugged dogmatism, 'that class should be frankly—*starkly*—vertical!'

'No, sir! That is impossible!'

Percy shrugged his shoulders loftily.

'You want a *horizontal* classification—like that of the sexes—upon the political plane, and that sort of class is no use.'

'No, sir! I want *no class at all*!'

There was a finality in this expression of the desideratum of Virgilio, of the syndic of postal workers, reaching him from the shrouded bed next his own, that caused Percy to pursue the subject no further. What was the use in talking to a brute? The lunch was where it should be, well down the trunk. Closing his eyes, he went to sleep.

Waking, and opening first his right eye, Percy perceived that Virgilio had removed his mosquito-curtain, and was smoking a cigarette. He had his history open.

With a bloodshot eye he was following the flight of the king to Varennes. He rode with Baillon on the heels of the fugitives. He knew that they could not escape him. Percy closed his eye again. He passed into a half-conscious doze.

'Percilito!' he heard. 'You are awake?'

He grunted angrily.

'What is it?'

'Nothing. Something had occurred to me.'

'Something is always occurring to you!' Percy muttered. He lay there without moving, and for a moment there was silence, except for the mosquitoes. Then he could scarcely believe his ears—for he heard Virgilio say, with great deliberation:

'I sometimes believe, Don Percy, that you are really a Fascist.'

Percy stiffened. Slowly he turned his head upon the pillow until both his eyes were trained upon the face of his neighbour.

'What is that?' he said heavily—still by no means sure that he had not after all been dreaming.

'I said sometimes I felt,' Virgilio repeated, 'that you were a Fascist.'

His ears had not deceived him, then! Now he had all his wits about him. In the face of an unprovoked charge of such gravity as this he must step warily. He cleared his throat and licked his lips.

'How do you make that out?' he asked off-handedly and in a thickish voice intended to convey that he was still more than half-asleep.

'I don't know. The things you say.'

'I talk a lot.'

'You don't seem to feel things, Percilito, like us. Not like a *sindicalista!*'

'No?'

'No. You feel them more like a Fascist.'

'Thank you, Virgilio! *Muchas gracias! Muchas gracias!'*

'*No hay de qué!*' responded placidly the prim-lipped Virgilio, from the syndicalized purlieus of Bilbao. Percy had always felt an invincible dislike for the Basques. And Virgilio was not a nicer Basque for being an ill-paid revolutionary agent.

One of the oddest things about Revolution was that it did not attract the *less* offensive national types. Nationality remained. It did not transform by magic this offensiveness into an acceptable something divorced from race and from nation.

'In what particularly do I *betray*'—Percy was ironically dignified—'*fascist* principles, my friend? Your idea interests me.'

'In what?'

'Yes—to come down to brass tacks, Muntán! No *feelings*, you know.'

'No feelings?'

'Yes. Something concrete, for once, if you don't mind.'

'You will not be offended, Don Percy?'

They had started *donning* each other, and going back to surnames—Percilito was to be a thing of the past, for the present.

'Not at all. Why should I be?'

'Are you sure? I feel you may.'

'You feel wrong,' Percy said energetically. 'Come on now. No wriggling out of it!'

There was a slight pause. British bluffness was nonplussing—Virgilio had nothing to meet it with, so it had to be isolated and left behind by an interval of silence, during which smoke poured out of the Basque's nose and mouth.

'Mirabeau was a freemason,' Virgilio remarked, as if imparting unwillingly a piece of disagreeable information, which he would have preferred to withhold.

'Well? What of it?'

'He is the type of man that you praise, Mirabeau.'

If this had not been such delicate ground, Percy would have smitten this devil hip and thigh, with a great onrush of withering words: as it was, he took a deep breath, and answered smoothly:

'But many of your leaders are freemasons.'

'No. None.'

'They are. I could name half a dozen.'

'None.'

'I could name a dozen.'

Virgilio waited for a name, or a dozen names. None were forthcoming. Percy knew better than that.

'Are you a freemason, Percy?' Virgilio asked.

Percy smiled, with easy scorn.

'No, I am not,' he said.

'You are not a mason, then?'

'No. What next? Get off the freemason lay. The only organization I belong to is the Communist party,' sternly and proudly he added.

Virgilio considered this statement very gravely.

'You have not the Communist mind,' he said at length.

'You think not?'

'I do not find in you the hatred I expect of the bourgeois.'

'I don't wear my hatred on my sleeve, as do some of my colleagues.'

Virgilio shrugged his shoulders.

'Your ideas of revolution are bourgeois. Administrative.'

'I am a practical man.'

'You believe in boss-rule. You are contemptuous of the people.'

'I will not have you say that!' Percy exclaimed, inflating his chest ominously, and panting a little. 'I *belong* to the people!'

Virgilio shrugged his shoulders again.

'All who are born in slums are not *proletarios.*'

'You do not need to tell me that!' exclaimed Percy. 'I was born in a slum.'

'I was born in a hospital for venereal diseases!' hissed back Virgilio. 'My mother was the lowest of prostitutes.' Virgilio's eyes flashed. He seemed to be accusing Percy of having connived at this situation. 'She had not even a name. I had *to steal* a name, to go about the world with!'

Percy was crushed. The wind had been completely taken out of his sails by this. He did not suppose it was true for a moment. But there was nothing more to be said. And his chest went back to its normal peace-time expansion—forty-two in place of forty-six, to which 'the slums' had carried it (*proletario* and proud of it!).

'Hardcaster is not *my* name either,' was all he could find to say.

'I didn't suppose it was,' said Virgilio contemptuously.

'It is Hardcastle. *Castillo duro.*'

'*Castillo?*' What had a 'castle' got to do with the social revolution, Virgilio seemed to want to know.

'Yes, I had to change it so as not to prejudice my mother's position in her slum: in case I "dishonoured" it!'

He tried to put great bitterness into this, but it fell flat. Virgilio pretended not to hear.

These biographical sallies and excursions had led them into a cul-de-sac—a cul-de-sac in a slum, dominated by a Lock Hospital. The Lock Hospital was an unassailable trump-card. There was no getting away from the Lock Hospital. And Percy gave up the attempt.

'You are an Anarchist at bottom, Virgilio,' said Percy at last in a palpably lame counter-attack. 'That is what you are. It is the old, old Spanish difficulty—you can never get away from it. The Spaniard spoils his socialism with his anarchism.'

'The Spaniard desires freedom. Not a new sort of slavery. He has had enough masters.'

Percy heaved himself impatiently upon the pillow.

'How often have I not heard that? You resent discipline.'

'You are English!' Virgilio retorted, with enough force to cause Percy to eye him warily, and resolve to bring this unprofitable conversation to an end. 'The English are not like us.'

'In what way do our problems differ?'

'The English are *"una nación de tenderos"*! You have the spirit of the little bourgeois. You cannot understand the Spanish.'

Percy laughed, a short bark of superior disdain. Whenever, upon one of the desiccated paths of Communist controversy, he encountered Don Quixote, he barked in his dry, unpleasant, fashion. For political purposes Cervantes's old lunatic must be bracketed with Saint John of the Cross and the Little Sisters of the Poor.

'We are climbing up on to our Rozinante, are we not? We become *nationalist*, I am afraid. I shall begin to think it is *you* who are the Fascist, Muntán!—Go to sleep, chico! Your brain needs a rest. You have begun contradicting yourself!'

And Percy crowed quickly, to clinch the matter. His face wore an expression of polite distaste, the lip curled up a little. He was displeased in the extreme. After this they talked less. The British syndicalist adopted a rather haughtier attitude towards his Biscayan ward-mate. He, too, had his Rozinante. (Britannia ruled the waves!) But he avoided certain areas of controversy. And he refused point-blank to discuss Thermidor—or the Mountain as against the Plain. And *l'Infâme* came in for more crushing and brow-beating than ever, now that others refused to take their reasonable share of sitting-on—by the big British big-wig of an imported politician; and indeed defied him, entrenched in their Lock Hospitals and armed with their false names.

Wyndham Lewis was in England during the war. This excerpt is from his novel The Revenge for Love *(written in 1937).*

AUTHORS TAKE SIDES

To the Writers and Poets of England, Scotland, Ireland, and Wales:

It is clear to many of us throughout the whole world that now, as certainly never before, we are determined or compelled, to take sides. The equivocal attitude, the Ivory Tower, the paradoxical, the ironic detachment, will no longer do.

We have seen murder and destruction by Fascism in Italy, in Germany—the organization there of social injustice and cultural death—and now revived, imperial Rome, abetted by international treachery, has conquered her place in the Abyssinian sun. The dark millions in the colonies are unavenged.

Today, the struggle is in Spain. Tomorrow it may be in other countries—our own. But there are some who, despite the martyrdom of Durango and Guernica, the enduring agony of Madrid, of Bilbao, and Germany's shelling of Almeria, are still in doubt, or who aver that it is possible that Fascism may be what it proclaims it is: 'the saviour of civilization'.

This is the question we are asking you: Are you for, or against, the legal Government and the People of Republican Spain? Are you for, or against, Franco and Fascism? For it is impossible for any longer to take no side.

Writers and Poets, we wish to print your answers. We wish the world to know what you, writers and poets, who are amongst the most sensitive instruments of a nation, feel.

Signed:

Paris—June 1937

Aragon	*Nancy Cunard*	*Pablo Neruda*
W. H. Auden	*Brian Howard*	*Ramon Sender*
José Bergamin	*Heinrich Mann*	*Stephen Spender*
Jean Richard Bloch	*Ivor Montagu*	*Tristan Tzara*

Samuel Beckett

¡UPTHEREPUBLIC!

C. Day Lewis

The struggle in Spain is part of a conflict going on now all over the world. I look upon it quite simply as a battle between light and darkness, of which only a blind man could be unaware. Both as a writer and as a member of the Communist Party I am bound to help in the fight against Fascism, which means certain destruction or living death for humanity.

．　．　．

T. S. Eliot

While I am naturally sympathetic, I still feel convinced that it is best that at least a few men of letters should remain isolated, and take no part in these collective activities.

Ezra Pound

Questionnaire an escape mechanism for young fools who are too cowardly to think; too lazy to investigate the nature of money, its mode of issue, the control of such issue by the Banque de France and the stank of England. You are all had. Spain is an emotional luxury to a gang of sap-headed dilettantes.

Evelyn Waugh

I know Spain only as a Tourist and a reader of the newspapers. I am no more impressed by the 'legality' of the Valencia Government than are English Communists by the legality of the Crown, Lords, and Commons. I believe it was a bad Government, rapidly deteriorating. If I were a Spaniard I should be fighting for General Franco. As an Englishman I am not in the predicament of choosing between two evils. I am not a Fascist nor shall I become one unless it were the only alternative to Marxism. It is mischievous to suggest that such a choice is imminent.

Louis MacNeice

I support the Valencia Government in Spain. Normally I would only support a cause because I hoped to get something out of it. Here the reason is stronger; if this cause is lost, nobody with civilized values may be able to get anything out of anything.

George Bernard Shaw

In Spain both the Right and the Left so thoroughly disgraced themselves in the turns they took in trying to govern their country before the Right revolted, that it is impossible to say which of them is the more incompetent. Spain must choose for itself: it is really not our business, though of course our Capitalist Government has done everything it possibly could to help General Franco. I as a Communist am generally on the Left; but that does not commit me to support the British Party Parliament system, and its continental imitations, of which I have the lowest opinion.

At present the Capitalist powers seem to have secured a victory over the General by what they call their non-interference, meaning their very active interference on his side; but it is unlikely that the last word will be with him. Meanwhile I shall not shout about it.

Aldous Huxley

My sympathies are, of course, with the Government side, especially the Anarchists; for Anarchism seems to me much more likely to lead to desirable social change than highly centralized, dictatorial Communism. As for 'taking sides'—the choice, it seems to me, is no longer between two users of violence, two systems of dictatorship. Violence and dictatorship cannot produce peace and liberty; they can only produce the results of violence and dictatorship, results with which history has made us only too sickeningly familiar.

The choice now is between militarism and pacifism. To me, the necessity of pacifism seems absolutely clear.

Ernest Hemingway

Just like any honest man I am against Franco and Fascism in Spain.

Theodore Dreiser

I am against Franco and Fascism generally. My reasons are that I believe that Fascism means a lack of intellectual freedom, a strongly militaristic and repressive social control joined seemingly with the continuance and strengthening of false religious, racial and economic ideologies, and generally speaking, the antithesis of any hope for equitable treatment which other forms of government at least pretend to offer the individual.

As regards Franco specifically, I believe he stands for the continuance of the Dark Age in Spain, where the Church and the soldiers control the wealth and welfare of the country, to the enslavement of the great mass of the people. I don't believe that Franco or the Fascists would ever let the Church itself regain the enormous economic power which the Church in Spain had, but I do believe that the Church under Franco would be the same as it is under Mussolini, an instrument through which the great mass of the people may be kept ignorant and subservient to a system which promises nothing for them.

W. H. Auden

I support the Valencia Government in Spain because its defeat by the forces of International Fascism would be a major disaster for Europe. It would make a European war more probable; and the spread of Fascist Ideology and practice to countries as yet comparatively free from them, which would inevitably follow upon a Fascist victory in Spain, would create an atmosphere in which the creative artist and all who care for justice, liberty, and culture would find it impossible to work or even exist.

To the Writers of America:

Fascism has appeared in the Western Hemisphere, not in the lurid imagination of alarmist prophets, but in the actual and openly acknowledged event. On Armistice Day the papers carried the news of the establishment in Brazil of a corporate state under dictatorial authority, and the abolition of parliamentary bodies elected by the people.

We know how German Fascism has murdered and destroyed, how Italian Fascism has conquered her place in the Abyssinian sun, how Japanese militarism fights in China her undeclared wars. We know how Fascist countries everywhere destroy civil liberties within their borders and ignore international law beyond them. Today the struggle rages east of us and west of us. Tomorrow it may be in our midst. It is constantly drawing nearer.

But there are some who, despite the martyrdom of Durango and Guernica, the enduring agony of Madrid, of Bilbao, the shelling of Almeria and Lerida, of Barcelona, and Valencia, are still in doubt, or who aver that it is possible that Fascism may be what it proclaims it is: the saviour of civilization.

We urge you to dispel the least shadow of that doubt. This is the question we would have you answer: 'Are you for, or are you against Franco and Fascism? Are you for, or are you against the legal government and the people of Republican Spain?' We desire to print your answers. We wish the whole country to know what is felt by the most sensitive instruments of the national life, you American writers. Your verdict has world importance.

Yours sincerely,
Donald Ogden Stewart
President, League of American Writers

Sherwood Anderson

Sure I am against all the damn Fascists or any other kind of dictator.

William Faulkner

I most sincerely wish to go on record as being unalterably opposed to Franco and Fascism, to all violations of the legal government and outrages against the people of Republican Spain.

Robinson Jeffers

You ask what I am for and what against in Spain. I would give my right hand, of course, to prevent the agony; I would not give a flick of my finger to help either side win.

. . .

John Steinbeck

Just returned from a little tour in the agricultural fields of California. We have our own Fascist groups out here. They haven't bombed open towns yet but in Salinas last year tear gas was thrown in a Union Hall and through the windows of working-men's houses. That's rather close, isn't it?

Your question as to whether I am for Franco is rather insulting. Have you seen anyone not actuated by greed who was for Franco? No, I'm not for Franco and his Moors and Italians and Germans. But some Americans are. Some Americans were for the Hessians England sent against our own revolutionary army. They were for the Hessians because they were selling things to them. The descendants of some of these Americans are still very rich and still touchy concerning the American Way, and our 'ancient liberties'. I am treasonable enough not to believe in the liberty of a man or a group to exploit, torment, or slaughter other men or groups. I believe in the despotism of human life and happiness against the liberty of money and possessions.

I. F. Stone

Only the writer who draws his sustenance from the caved-in teat of a decayed past can be a Fascist. Fascism is capitalism seeking by brutality to evade the logic that moves mankind inexorably towards the common-sense solution of the paradox that puts want amid plenty, idle men beside idle factories, underfed children in a land of rotting crops. Fascism, by its very nature, must be anti-rational and anti-humane.

Criminal disunity among liberals and the Left helped Fascism to victory in Italy and Germany. The Popular

Front has made it possible for the people of Spain to fight the greatest battle against Fascism the world has yet seen. It is not strange that the allies of Spanish Fascism are to be found in brown shirt and in black shirt in the most backward section of the Catholic Church, among ignorant Moors and in those refined upper circles of the British aristocracy so delicately bred that they prefer the murder of children in Barcelona to the loss of a penny on their profits from Rio Tinto.

If the Spanish people win, the forces of Fascism will be set back the world over. Should the Loyalists lose, we may expect a tidal wave of reaction, obscurantism, race hatred, and thuggery, menacing our own lives and our own homes. We must never forget that the barricades in Madrid are barricades everywhere—in defence of freedom, of culture, and of humanity.

The above answers are excerpted from two questionnaires: The first, Authors Take Sides, *was written in Paris and published in London in 1937. The second,* Writers Take Sides, *was published by Donald Ogden Stewart and the League of American Writers in New York in 1938.*

STEPHEN SPENDER

Poems About the Spanish Civil War

THE ROOM ABOVE THE SQUARE

The light in the window seemed perpetual
When you stayed in the high room for me;
It glowed above the trees through leaves
Like my certainty.

The light is fallen and you are hidden
In sunbright peninsulas of the sword:
Torn like leaves through Europe is the peace
That through us flowed.

Now I climb alone to the high room
Above the darkened square
Where among stones and roots, the other
Unshattered lovers are.

THOUGHTS DURING AN AIR RAID

Of course, the entire effort is to put oneself
Outside the ordinary range
Of what are called statistics. A hundred are killed
In the outer suburbs. Well, well, one carries on.
So long as this thing 'I' is propped up on
The girdered bed which seems so like a hearse,
In the hotel bedroom with the wall-paper
Blowing smoke-wreaths of roses, one can ignore
The pressure of those names under the fingers
Indented by lead type on newsprint,
In the bar, the marginal wailing wireless.
Yet supposing that a bomb should dive
Its nose right through this bed, with one upon it?
The thought's obscene. Still, there are many
For whom one's loss would illustrate
The 'impersonal' use indeed. The essential is
That every 'one' should remain separate
Propped up under roses, and no one suffer
For his neighbour. Then horror is postponed
Piecemeal for each, until it settles on him
That wreath of incommunicable grief
Which is all mystery or nothing.

TWO ARMIES

Deep in the winter plain, two armies
Dig their machinery, to destroy each other.
Men freeze and hunger. No one is given leave
On either side, except the dead, and wounded.
These have their leave; while new battalions wait
On time at last to bring them violent peace.

All have become so nervous and so cold
That each man hates the cause and distant words
That brought him here, more terribly than bullets.
Once a boy hummed a popular marching song,
Once a novice hand flapped their salute;
The voice was choked, the lifted hand fell,
Shot through the wrist by those of his own side.

From their numb harvest, all would flee, except
For discipline drilled once in an iron school
Which holds them at the point of the revolver.
Yet when they sleep, the images of home
Ride wishing horses of escape
Which herd the plain in a mass unspoken poem.

Finally, they cease to hate: for although hate
Bursts from the air and whips the earth with hail
Or shoots it up in fountains to marvel at,
And although hundreds fall, who can connect
The inexhaustible anger of the guns
With the dumb patience of those tormented animals?

Clean silence drops at night, when a little walk
Divides the sleeping armies, each
Huddled in linen woven by remote hands.
When the machines are stilled, a common suffering
Whitens the air with breath and makes both one
As though these enemies slept in each other's arms.

Only the lucid friend to aerial raiders
The brilliant pilot moon, stares down
Upon this plain she makes a shining bone
Cut by the shadows of many thousand bones.
Where amber clouds scatter on No-Man's-Land
She regards death and time throw up
The furious words and minerals which destroy.

ULTIMA RATIO REGUM

The guns spell money's ultimate reason
In letters of lead on the Spring hillside.
But the boy lying dead under the olive trees
Was too young and too silly
To have been notable to their important eye.
He was a better target for a kiss.

When he lived, tall factory hooters never summoned him
Nor did restaurant plate-glass doors revolve to wave
    him in
His name never appeared in the papers.
The world maintained its traditional wall
Round the dead with their gold sunk deep as a well,
Whilst his life, intangible as a Stock Exchange rumour,
    drifted outside.

O too lightly he threw down his cap
One day when the breeze threw petals from the trees.
The unflowering wall sprouted with guns,
Machine-gun anger quickly scythed the grasses;
Flags and leaves fell from hands and branches;
The tweed cap rotted in the nettles.

Consider his life which was valueless
In terms of employment, hotel ledgers, news files.
Consider. One bullet in ten thousand kills a man.
Ask. Was so much expenditure justified
On the death of one so young, and so silly
Lying under the olive trees, O world, O death?

A STOPWATCH AND AN ORDNANCE MAP

to Samuel Barber

A stopwatch and an ordnance map.
At five a man fell to the ground
And the watch flew off his wrist
Like a moon struck from the earth
Marking a blank time that stares
On the tides of change beneath.
All under the olive trees.

A stopwatch and an ordnance map.
He stayed faithfully in that place
From his living comrade split
By dividers of the bullet
Opening wide the distances
Of his final loneliness.
All under the olive trees.

A stopwatch and an ordnance map.
And the bones are fixed at five
Under the moon's timelessness;
But another who lives on
Wears within his heart for ever
Space split open by the bullet.
All under the olive trees.

IN NO MAN'S LAND

Only the world changes, and time its tense
Against the creeping inches of whose moons
He launches his rigid continual present.

The grass will grow its summer beard and beams
Of sunlight melt the iron slumber
Where soldiers lie locked in their final dreams.

His corpse be covered with the white December
And roots push through his skin as through a drum
When the years and fields forget, but the bones
    remember.

THE COWARD

Under the olive trees, from the ground
Grows this flower, which is a wound.
This is wiser to ignore
Than the heroes' sunset fire
Raging with flags on the world's shore.
These blood-dark petals have no name
But the coward's nameless shame.
Here one died, not like a soldier
Of lead, but of rings of terror.
His final moment was the birth
Of naked revelatory truth:
He saw the flagship at the quay,
His mother's care, his lover's kiss,
The white accompaniment of spray,
Lead to the bullet and to this.
Flesh, bone, muscle, eyes,
Built in their noble tower of lies,
Scattered on the icy breeze
Him their false promises betrayed.
All the visions in one instant
Changed to this fixed continual present
Under the grey olive trees.
There's no excuse here for excuse.
Nothing can count but love, to pour
Out its useless comfort here.
To populate his loneliness
And to bring his ghost release
Love and pity dare not cease
For a lifetime, at the least.

FALL OF A CITY

All the posters on the walls,
All the leaflets in the streets
Are mutilated, destroyed, or run in rain,
Their words blotted out with tears,
Skins peeling from their bodies
In the victorious hurricane.

All the names of heroes in the hall
Where the feet thundered and the bronze throats roared
Fox and LORCA claimed as history on the walls,
Are now furiously deleted
Or to dust surrender their gold
From praise excluded.

All the badges and salutes
Torn from lapels and from hands,
Are thrown away with human sacks they wore,
Or in the deepest bed of mind
They are washed over with a smile
Which launches the victors where they win.

All the lessons learned, unlearnt;
The young, who learned to read, now blind
Their eyes with an archaic film;
The peasant relapses to a stumbling tune
Following the donkey's bray;
These only remember to forget.

But somewhere some word presses
In the high door of a skull, and in some corner
Of an irrefrangible eye
Some old man's memory jumps to a child
—Spark from the days of liberty.
And the child hoards it like a bitter toy.

PORT BOU

As a child holds a pet
Arms clutching but with hands that do not join
And the coiled animal looks through the gap
To outer freedom animal air,
So the earth-and-rock arms of this small harbour
Embrace but do not encircle the sea
Which, through a gap, vibrates into the ocean,
Where dolphins swim and liners throb.
In the bright winter sunlight I sit on the parapet
Of a bridge; my circling arms rest on a newspaper
And my mind is empty as the glittering stone
While I search for an image
(The one written above) and the words (written above)
To set down the childish headlands of Port Bou.
A lorry halts beside me with creaking brakes
And I look up at warm downwards-looking faces
Of militiamen staring at my (French) newspaper.
'How do they write of our struggle over the frontier?'
I hold out the paper, but they cannot read it,
They want speech and to offer cigarettes.
In their waving flag-like faces the war finds peace. The
    famished mouths
Of rusted carbines lean against their knees,
Like leaning, rust-coloured, fragile reeds.
Wrapped in cloth—old granny in a shawl—
The stuttering machine-gun rests.
They shout—salute back as the truck jerks forward
Over the vigorous hill, beyond the headland.
An old man passes, his mouth dribbling,

From three rusted teeth, he shoots out: 'pom-pom-pom'.
The children run after; and, more slowly, the women;
Clutching their skirts, trail over the horizon.
Now Port Bou is empty, for the firing practice.
I am left alone on the parapet at the exact centre
Above the river trickling through the gulley, like that
    old man's saliva.
The exact centre, solitary as the bull's eye in a target.
Nothing moves against the background of stage-scenery
    houses
Save the skirring mongrels. The firing now begins
Across the harbour mouth, from headland to headland,
White flecks of foam whipped by lead from the sea.
An echo spreads its cat-o'-nine tails
Thrashing the flanks of neighbour hills.
My circling arms rest on the newspaper,
My mind is paper on which dust and words sift,
I assure myself the shooting is only for practice
But I am the coward of cowards. The machine-gun
    stitches
My intestines with a needle, back and forth;
The solitary, spasmodic, white puffs from the carbines
Draw fear in white threads back and forth through my
    body.

TO A SPANISH POET

for Manuel Altolaguirre

You stared out of the window on the emptiness
Of a world exploding;
Stones and rubble thrown upwards in a fountain
Blown to one side by the wind.
Every sensation except being alone
Drained out of your mind.
There was no fixed object for the eye to fix on.
You became a child again
Who sees for the first time how the worst things happen.

Then, stupidly, the stucco pigeon
On the gable roof that was your ceiling,
Parabolized before your window
Uttering (you told me later!) a loud coo.
Alone to your listening self, you told the joke.
Everything in the room broke.
But you remained whole,
Your own image unbroken in your glass soul.

Having heard this all from you, I see you now
—White astonishment haloing irises
Which still retain in their centres
Black laughter of black eyes.
Laughter reverberant through stories
Of an aristocrat lost in the hills near Malaga
Where he had got out of his carriage
And, for a whole week, followed, on foot, a partridge.
Stories of that general, broken-hearted
Because he'd failed to breed a green-eyed bull.

But reading the news, my imagination breeds
The penny-dreadful fear that you are dead.

Well, what of this journalistic dread?

Perhaps it is we—the living—who are dead
We of a world that revolves and dissolves
While we set the steadfast corpse under the earth's lid.
The eyes push irises above the grave
Reaching to the stars, which draw down nearer,
Staring through a rectangle of night like black glass,
Beyond these daylight comedies of falling plaster.

Your heart looks through the breaking ribs—
Oiled axle through revolving spokes.
Unbroken blood of the swift wheel,
You stare through centrifugal bones
Of the revolving and dissolving world.

*Stephen Spender was a leading supporter of the Republic,
speaking publicly and writing for a variety of journals and
magazines. The poems he wrote during that time (1936–39)
are collected here.*

LUIS BUÑUEL

The Civil War

In July 1936, Franco arrived in Spain with his Moroccan troops and the firm intention of demolishing the Republic and re-establishing "order." My wife and son had gone back to Paris the month before, and I was alone in Madrid. Early one morning, I was jolted awake by a series of explosions and cannon fire; a Republican plane was bombing the Montaña army barracks.

At this time, all the barracks in Spain were filled with soldiers. A group of Falangists had ensconced themselves in the Montaña and had been firing from its windows for several days, wounding many civilians. On the morning of July 18, groups of workers, armed and supported by Azaña's Republican assault troops, attacked the barracks. It was all over by ten o'clock, the rebel officers and Falangists executed. The war had begun.

It was hard to believe. Listening to the distant machine-gun fire from my balcony, I watched a Schneider cannon roll by in the street below, pulled by a couple of workers and some gypsies. The revolution we'd felt

gathering force for so many years, and which I personally had so ardently desired, was now going on before
my eyes. All I felt was shock.

Two weeks later, Elie Faure, the famous art historian
and an ardent supporter of the Republican cause, came
to Madrid for a few days. I went to visit him one morning at his hotel and can still see him standing at his
window in his long underwear, watching the demonstrations in the street below and weeping at the sight of
the people in arms. One day, we watched a hundred
peasants marching by, four abreast, some armed with
hunting rifles and revolvers, some with sickles and pitchforks. In an obvious effort at discipline, they were trying
very hard to march in step. Faure and I both wept.

It seemed as if nothing could defeat such a deep-seated
popular force, but the joy and enthusiasm that colored
those early days soon gave way to arguments, disorganization, and uncertainty—all of which lasted until
November 1936, when an efficient and disciplined Republican organization began to emerge. I make no
claims to writing a serious account of the deep gash
that ripped through my country in 1936. I'm not a
historian, and I'm certainly not impartial. I can only
try to describe what I saw and what I remember. At the
same time, I do see those first months in Madrid very
clearly. Theoretically, the city was still in the hands
of the Republicans, but Franco had already reached
Toledo, after occupying other cities like Salamanca and
Burgos. Inside Madrid, there was constant sniping by
Fascist sympathizers. The priests and the rich landowners—in other words, those with conservative lean-
ings, whom we assumed would support the Falange—
were in constant danger of being executed by the Republicans. The moment the fighting began, the anar-

chists liberated all political prisoners and immediately incorporated them into the ranks of the Confederación Nacional de Trabajo, which was under the direct control of the anarchist federation. Certain members of this federation were such extremists that the mere presence of a religious icon in someone's room led automatically to Casa Campo, the public park on the outskirts of the city where the executions took place. People arrested at night were always told that they were going to "take a little walk."

It was advisable to use the intimate *"tu"* form of address for everyone, and to add an energetic *compañero* whenever you spoke to an anarchist, or a *camarada* to a Communist. Most cars carried a couple of mattresses tied to the roof as protection against snipers. It was dangerous even to hold out your hand to signal a turn, as the gesture might be interpreted as a Fascist salute and get you a fast round of gunfire. The *señoritos,* the sons of "good" families, wore old caps and dirty clothes in order to look as much like workers as they could, while on the other side the Communist party recommended that the workers wear white shirts and ties.

Ontañon, who was a friend of mine and a well-known illustrator, told me about the arrest of Sáenz de Heredia, a director who'd worked for me on *La hija de Juan Simón* and *Quién me quiere a mí?* Sáenz, Primo de Rivera's first cousin, had been sleeping on a park bench because he was afraid to go home, but despite his precautions he had been picked up by a group of Socialists and was now awaiting execution because of his fatal family connections. When I heard about this, I immediately went to the Rotpence Studios, where I found that the employees, as in many other enterprises, had formed a council and were holding a meeting. When I asked how Sáenz was, they all replied that he was "just fine," that they had "nothing against him." I begged them to appoint a delegation to go with me to the Calle de Marqués de Riscál, where he was being held, and to tell the Socialists what they'd just told me. A few men with rifles agreed, but when we arrived, all we found was one guard sitting at the gate with his rifle lying casually in his lap. In as threatening a voice as I could muster, I demanded to see his superior, who turned out to be a lieutenant I'd had dinner with the evening before.

"Well, Buñuel," he said calmly, "what're you doing here?"

I explained that we really couldn't execute *everyone,* that of course we were all very aware of Sáenz's relationship to Primo de Rivera, but that the director had always acted perfectly correctly. The delegates from the studio also spoke in his favor, and eventually he was released, only to slip away to France and later join the Falange. After the war, he went back to directing movies, and even made a film glorifying Franco! The last I saw of him was at a long, nostalgic lunch we had together in the 1950s at the Cannes Festival.

During this time, I was very friendly with Santiago Carrillo, the secretary of the United Socialist Youth. Finding myself unarmed in a city where people were firing on each other from all sides, I went to see Carrillo and asked for a gun.

"There are no more," he replied, opening his empty drawer.

After a prodigious search, I finally got someone to give me a rifle. I remember one day when I was with some friends on the Plaza de la Independencia and the shooting began. People were firing from rooftops, from windows, from behind parked cars. It was bedlam, and there I was, behind a tree with my rifle, not knowing where to fire. Why bother having a gun, I wondered, and rushed off to give it back.

The first three months were the worst, mostly because of the total absence of control. I, who had been such an ardent subversive, who had so desired the overthrow of the established order, now found myself in the middle of a volcano, and I was afraid. If certain exploits seemed to me both absurd and glorious—like the workers who climbed into a truck one day and drove out to the monument to the Sacred Heart of Jesus about twenty kilometers south of the city, formed a firing squad, and executed the statue of Christ—I nonetheless couldn't stomach the summary executions, the looting, the criminal acts. No sooner had the people risen and seized power than they split into factions and began tearing one another to pieces. This insane and indiscriminate settling of accounts made everyone forget the essential reasons for the war.

I went to nightly meetings of the Association of Writers and Artists for the Revolution, where I saw most of my friends—Alberti, Bergamín, the journalist Corpus Varga, and the poet Altolaguirre, who believed in God and who later produced my *Mexican Bus Ride*. The group was constantly erupting in passionate and interminable arguments, many of which concerned whether we should just act spontaneously or try to organize ourselves. As usual, I was torn between my intellectual (and emotional) attraction to anarchy and my fundamental need for order and peace. And there we sat, in a life-and-death situation, but spending all our time constructing theories.

Franco continued to advance. Certain towns and cities remained loyal to the Republic, but others surrendered to him without a struggle. Fascist repression was pitiless; anyone suspected of liberal tendencies was summarily executed. But instead of trying to form an organization, we debated—while the anarchists persecuted priests. I can still hear the old cry: "Come down and see. There's a dead priest in the street." As anticlerical as I was, I couldn't condone this kind of massacre, even though the priests were not exactly innocent bystanders. They took up arms like everybody else, and did a fair bit of sniping from their bell towers. We even saw Dominicans with machine guns. A few of the clergy joined the Republican side, but most went over to the Fascists. The war spared no one, and it was impossible to remain neutral, to declare allegiance to the utopian illusion of a *tercera España*.

Some days, I was very frightened. I lived in an extremely bourgeois apartment house and often wondered what would happen if a wild bunch of anarchists suddenly broke into my place in the middle of the night to "take me for a walk." Would I resist? How could I? What could I say to them?

The city was rife with stories; everyone had one. I remember hearing about some nuns in a convent in Madrid who were on their way to chapel and stopped in front of the statue of the Virgin holding the baby Jesus in her arms. With a hammer and chisel, the mother superior removed the child and carried it away.

"We'll bring him back," she told the Virgin, "when we've won the war."

The Republican camp was riddled with dissension. The main goal of both Communists and Socialists was to win the war, while the anarchists, on the other hand, considered the war already won and had begun to organize their ideal society.

"We've started a commune at Torrelodones," Gil Bel, the editor of the labor journal *El Sindicalista*, told me one day at the Café Castilla. "We already have twenty houses, all occupied. You ought to take one."

I was beside myself with rage and surprise. Those houses belonged to people who'd fled or been executed. And as if that weren't enough, Torrelodones stood at the foot of the Sierra de Guadarrama, only a few kilometers from the Fascist front lines. Within shooting distance of Franco's army, the anarchists were calmly laying out their utopia.

On another occasion, I was having lunch in a restaurant with the musician Remacha, one of the directors of the Filmófono Studios where I'd once worked. The son of the restaurant owner had been seriously wounded fighting the Falangists in the Sierra de Guadarrama. Suddenly, several armed anarchists burst into the restaurant yelling, *"Salud compañeros!"* and shouting for wine. Furious, I told them they should be in the mountains fighting instead of emptying the wine cellar of a good man whose son was fighting for his life in a hospital. They sobered up quickly and left, taking the bottles with them, of course.

Every evening, whole brigades of anarchists came down out of the hills to loot the hotel wine cellars. Their behavior pushed many of us into the arms of the Communists. Few in number at the beginning of the war, they were nonetheless growing stronger with each passing day. Organized and disciplined, focused on the war itself, they seemed to me then, as they do now, irreproachable. It was sad but true that the anarchists hated them more than they hated the Fascists. This animosity had begun several years before the war when, in 1935, the Federación Anarquista Ibérica (FAI) announced a general strike among construction workers. The anarchist Ramón Acin, who financed *Las Hurdes,* told me about the time a Communist delegation went to see the head of the strike committee.

"There are three police stoolies in your ranks," they told him, naming names.

"So what?" the anarchist retorted. "We know all about it, but we like stoolies better than Communists."

Despite my ideological sympathies with the anarchists, I couldn't stand their unpredictable and fanatical behavior. Sometimes, it was sufficient merely to be an engineer or to have a university degree to be taken away to Casa Campo. When the Republican government moved its headquarters from Madrid to Barcelona because of the Fascist advance, the anarchists threw up a barricade near Cuenca on the only road that hadn't been cut. In Barcelona itself, they liquidated the director and the engineers in a metallurgy factory in order to prove that the factory could function perfectly well when run by the workers. Then they built a tank and proudly showed it to a Soviet delegate. (When he asked for a parabellum and fired at it, it fell apart.)

Despite all the other theories, a great many people thought that the anarchists were responsible for the death of Durutti, who was shot while getting out of his car on the Calle de la Princesa, on his way to try to ease the situation at the university, which was under siege. They were the kind of fanatics who named their daughters Acracia (Absence of Power) or Fourteenth September, and couldn't forgive Durutti the discipline he'd imposed on his troops.

We also feared the arbitrary actions of the POUM (Partido Obrero de Unificación Marxista), which was theoretically a Trotskyite group. Members of this movement, along with anarchists from the FAI, built barricades in May 1937 in the streets of Barcelona against the Republican army, which then had to fight its own allies in order to get through.

My friend Claudio de la Torre lived in an isolated house outside of Madrid. His grandfather had been a freemason, the quintessential abomination in the eyes of the Fascists. In fact, they despised freemasons as heartily as they did the Communists. Claudio had an excellent cook whose fiancé was fighting with the anarchists. One day I went to his house for lunch, and suddenly, out there in the open country, a POUM car drove up. I was very nervous, because the only papers I had on me were Socialist and Communist, which meant less than nothing to the POUM. When the car pulled up to the door, the driver leaned out and . . . asked for directions. Claudio gave them readily enough, and we both heaved a great sigh of relief as he drove away.

All in all, the dominant feeling was one of insecurity and confusion, aggravated, despite the threat of fascism on our very doorstep, by endless internal conflicts and diverging tendencies. As I watched the realization of an old dream, all I felt was sadness.

And then one day I learned of Lorca's death, from a Republican who'd somehow managed to slip through the lines. Shortly before *Un Chien andalou*, Lorca and I had had a falling-out; later, thin-skinned Andalusian that he was, he thought (or pretended to think) that the film was actually a personal attack on him.

"Buñuel's made a little film, just like that!" he used to say, snapping his fingers. "It's called *An Andalusian Dog*, and I'm the dog!"

By 1934, however, we were the best of friends once again; and despite the fact that I sometimes thought he was a bit too fond of public adulation, we spent a great deal of time together. With Ugarte, we often drove out into the mountains to relax for a few hours in the Gothic solitude of El Paular. The monastery itself was in ruins, but there were a few spartan rooms reserved for people from the Fine Arts Institute. If you brought your own sleeping bag, you could even spend the night.

It was difficult, of course, to have serious discussions about painting and poetry while the war raged around us. Four days before Franco's arrival, Lorca, who never got excited about politics, suddenly decided to leave for Granada, his native city.

"Federico," I pleaded, trying to talk him out of it. "Horrendous things are happening. You can't go down there now; it's safer to stay right here."

He paid no attention to any of us, and left, tense and frightened, the following day. The news of his death was a terrific shock. Of all the human beings I've ever known, Federico was the finest. I don't mean his plays or his poetry; I mean him personally. He was his own masterpiece. Whether sitting at the piano imitating Chopin, improvising a pantomime, or acting out a scene from a play, he was irresistible. He read beautifully, and he had passion, youth, and joy. When I first met him, at the Residencia, I was an unpolished rustic, interested primarily in sports. He transformed me, introduced me to a wholly different world. He was like a flame.

His body was never found. Rumors about his death circulated freely, and Dali even made the ignoble suggestion that there'd been some homosexual foul play involved. The truth is that Lorca died because he was a poet. "Death to the intelligentsia" was a favorite wartime slogan. When he got to Granada, he apparently stayed with the poet Rosales, a Falangist whose family was friendly with Lorca's. I guess he thought he was safe with Rosales, but a group of men (no one knows who they were, and it doesn't really matter, anyway) led by someone called Alonso appeared one night, arrested him, and drove him away in a truck with some workers. Federico was terrified of suffering and death. I can imagine what he must have felt, in the middle of the night in a truck that was taking him to an olive grove to be shot. I think about it often.

At the end of September, the Republican minister of foreign affairs, Alvarez del Vayo, asked to see me. Curious, I went to his office and was told only that I'd find out everything I wanted to know when I got to Geneva. I left Madrid in an overcrowded train and found myself sitting next to a POUM commander, who kept shouting that the Republican government was garbage and had to be wiped out at any cost. (Ironically, I was to use this commander later, as a spy, when I worked in Paris.) When I changed trains in Barcelona, I ran into José Bergamín and Muñoz Suaï, who were going to Geneva with several students to attend a political convention. They asked me what kind of papers I was carrying.

"But you'll never get across the border," Suaï cried, when I told him. "You need a visa from the anarchists to do that!"

The first thing I saw when we arrived at Port Bou was

a group of soldiers ringing the station, and a table where three somber-faced anarchists, led by a bearded Italian, were holding court like a panel of judges.

"You can't cross here," they told me when I showed them my papers.

Now the Spanish language is capable of more scathing blasphemies than any other language I know. Curses elsewhere are typically brief and punctuated by other comments, but the Spanish curse tends to take the form of a long speech in which extraordinary vulgarities— referring chiefly to the Virgin Mary, the Apostles, God, Christ, and the Holy Spirit, not to mention the Pope— are strung end to end in a series of impressive scatological exclamations. In fact, blasphemy in Spain is truly an art; in Mexico, for instance, I never heard a proper curse, whereas in my native land, a good one lasts for at least three good-sized sentences. (When circumstances require, it can become a veritable hymn.)

It was with a curse of this kind, uttered in all its seemly intensity, that I regaled the three anarchists from Port Bou. When I'd finished, they stamped my papers and I crossed the border. (What I've said about the importance of the Spanish curse is no exaggeration; in certain old Spanish cities, you can still see signs like "No Begging or Blaspheming—Subject to Fine or Imprisonment" on the main gates. Sadly, when I returned to Spain in 1960, the curse seemed much rarer; or perhaps it was only my hearing.)

In Geneva, I had a fast twenty-minute meeting with the minister, who asked me to go to Paris and start work for the new ambassador, who turned out to be my friend Araquistán, a former journalist, writer, and left-wing Socialist. Apparently, he needed men he could trust. I stayed in Paris until the end of the war; I had an office

on the rue de la Pépinière and was officially responsible
for cataloguing the Republican propaganda films made
in Spain. In fact, however, my job was somewhat more
complicated. On the one hand, I was a kind of protocol
officer, responsible for organizing dinners at the embassy, which meant making sure that André Gide was
not seated next to Louis Aragon. On the other hand, I
was supposed to oversee "news and propaganda." This
job required that I travel—to Switzerland, Antwerp
(where the Belgian Communists gave us their total support), Stockholm, London—drumming up support for
various Republican causes. I also went to Spain from
time to time, carrying suitcases stuffed with tracts that
had been printed in Paris. Thanks to the complicity of
certain sailors, our tracts once traveled to Spain on a
German ship.

While the French government steadfastly refused to
compromise or to intervene on behalf of the Republic,
a move that would certainly have changed the direction of things, the French people, particularly the
workers who belonged to the Confédération Générale
de Travail, helped us enormously. It wasn't unusual,
for instance, for a railroad employee or a taxi driver to
come see me and tell me that two Fascists had arrived
the previous night on the eight-fifteen train and had
gone to such-and-such a hotel. I passed all information
of this kind directly to Araquistán, who was proving to
be by far our most efficient ambassador.

The nonintervention of France and the other democratic powers was fatal to the Republican cause. Although Roosevelt did declare his support, he ceded to
the pressure from his Catholic constituency and did not
intervene. Neither did Léon Blum in France. We'd
never hoped for direct participation, but we had thought

that France, like Germany and Italy, would at least authorize the transport of arms and "volunteers." In fact, the fate of Spanish refugees in France was nothing short of disastrous. Usually, they were simply picked up at the border and thrown directly into camps. Later, many of them fell into the hands of the Nazis and perished in Germany, mainly in Mauthausen.

The International Brigades, organized and trained by the Communists, were the only ones who gave us real aid, but there were others who simply appeared on their own, ready to fight. Homage should also be paid to Malraux, albeit some of the pilots he sent were little more than mercenaries. In my Paris office, I issued safe-conduct passes to Hemingway, Dos Passos, and Joris Ivens, so they could make a documentary on the Republican army.

There was a good deal of frustrating intrigue going on while we were making a propaganda film in Spain with the help of two Russian cameramen. This particular film was to have worldwide distribution, but after I returned to Paris, I heard nothing for several months on the progress of the shoot. Finally, I made an appointment with the head of the Soviet trade delegation, who kept me waiting for an hour until I began shouting at his secretary. The man finally received me icily.

"And what are *you* doing in Paris?" he asked testily.

I retorted that he had absolutely no right to evaluate my activities, that I only followed orders, and that I only wanted to know what had happened to the film. He refused to answer my question and showed me rather unceremoniously to the door. As soon as I got back to my office, I wrote four letters—one to *L'Humanité,* one to *Pravda*, one to the Russian ambassador, and the last to the Spanish minister—denouncing what seemed to be sabotage inside the Soviet trade delegation itself (a charge that was eventually confirmed by friends in the French Communist Party, who told me that it was "the same all over"). It seemed that the Soviet Union had enemies, even within its own official circles, and indeed, some time later, the head of the delegation became one of the victims of the Stalinist purges.

Another strange story, which sheds a curious light on the French police (not to mention police all over the world), concerns three mysterious bombs. One day, a young and very elegant Colombian walked into my office. He'd asked to see the military attaché, but since we no longer had one, I suppose someone thought I was the next best thing. He put a small suitcase on my desk, and when he opened it, there lay three little bombs.

"They may be small," he said to me, "but they're powerful. They're the ones we used in the attacks on the Spanish consulate in Perpignan and on the Bordeaux-Marseille train."

Dumbfounded, I asked him what he wanted and why he'd come to me. He replied that he had no intention of hiding his Fascist sympathies (he was a member of the Condor Legion) but that he was doing this because he despised his superior!

"I want him arrested," he said simply. "Why is none of your business. But if you want to meet him, come to La Coupole tomorrow at five o'clock. He'll be the man on my right. I'll just leave these with you, then."

As soon as he'd gone, I told Araquistán, who phoned the prefect of police. When their bombs experts got through with their analysis, it turned out that our terrorist had been right; they were more potent than any others of that size.

The next day, I invited the ambassador's son and an

actress friend of mine to have a drink with me at La Coupole. The Colombian was exactly where he said he'd be, sitting on the terrace with a group of people. And as incredible as it may sound, I knew the man on his right, and so did my friend. He was a Latin American actor, and we all shook hands quite amicably as we walked by. (His treacherous colleague never moved a muscle.)

Since I now knew the name of the leader of this terrorist group, as well as the hotel in Paris where he lived, I contacted the prefect, who was a Socialist, as soon as I got back to the embassy. He assured me that they'd pick him right up; but time went by, and nothing happened. Later, when I ran into the boss sitting happily with his friends at the Select on the Champs-Elysées, I wept with rage. What kind of world is this? I asked myself. Here's a known criminal, and the police don't want any part of him!

Shortly afterward, I heard from my Colombian informant again, who told me that his leader would be at our embassy the next day applying for a visa to Spain. Once again, he was correct. The actor had a diplomatic passport and got his visa with no trouble whatsoever. On his way to Madrid, however, he was arrested at the border by the Republican police, who'd been warned ahead of time; but he was released almost immediately on the protest of his government. He went on to Madrid, carried out his mission, and then calmly returned to Paris. Was he invulnerable? What kind of protection did he have? I was desperate to know.

Around that time, I left on a mission to Stockholm, where I read in a newspaper that a bomb had leveled a small apartment building near the Etoile that had been the headquarters of a labor union. I remember the article saying quite precisely that the bomb was so powerful the building had simply crumbled to dust, and that two agents had died in the blast. It was obvious which terrorist had done the job.

Again, nothing happened. The man continued to pursue his activities, protected by the careful indifference of the French police, who seemed to support whomever had the upper hand. At the end of the war, the actor, a member of the Fifth Column, was decorated for his services by Franco.

While my terrorist was cheerfully going about his dirty work in Paris, I was being violently attacked by the French right wing, who—believe it or not—had not forgotten *L'Age d'or*. They wrote about my taste for profanity and my "anal complex," and the newspaper *Gringoire* (or was it *Candide*?) reminded its readers that I'd come to Paris several years before in an effort to "corrupt French youth."

One day, Breton came to see me at the embassy.

"Mon cher ami," he began, "there seem to be some disagreeable rumors about the Republicans' executing Péret because he belonged to POUM."

POUM had inspired some adherence among the surrealists. In fact, Benjamin Péret had left for Barcelona, where he could be seen every day on the Plaza Cataluña surrounded by people from POUM. On Breton's request, I asked some questions and learned that Péret had gone to the Aragón front in Huesca; apparently, he'd also criticized the behavior of certain POUM members so openly and vociferously that many had announced their firm intention of shooting him. I guaranteed Breton that Péret hadn't been executed by the Republicans, however, and he returned to France soon afterward, safe and sound.

From time to time, I met Dali for lunch at the Rôtisserie Périgourdine on the place St.-Michel. One day, he made me a bizarre offer.

"I can introduce you to an enormously rich Englishman," he said. "He's on your side, and he wants to give you a bomber!"

The Englishman, Edward James, had just bought all of Dali's 1938 output, and did indeed want to give the Republicans an ultramodern bomber which was then hidden in a Czechoslovakian airport. Knowing that the Republic was dramatically short of air strength, he was making us this handsome present—in exchange for a few masterpieces from the Prado. He wanted to set up an exhibition in Paris, as well as in other cities in France; the paintings would be placed under the warranty of the International Tribunal at The Hague, and after the war there would be two options: If the Republicans won, the paintings would be returned to the Prado, but if Franco was victorious, they'd remain the property of the Republican government in exile.

I conveyed this unusual proposition to Alvarez del Vayo, who admitted that a bomber would be very welcome, but that wild horses couldn't make him take paintings out of the Prado. "What would they say about us?" he demanded. "What would the press make of this? That we traded our patrimony for arms? No, no, it's impossible. Let's have no further talk about it."

(Edward James is still alive and is the owner of several châteaus, not to mention a large ranch in Mexico.)

My secretary was the daughter of the treasurer of the French Communist party. He'd belonged to the infamous Bande à Bonnot, and his daughter remembers taking walks as a child on the arm of the notorious Raymond-la-Science. I myself knew two old-timers from the band—Rirette Maîtrejean and the gentleman who did cabaret numbers and called himself the "innocent convict." One day, a communiqué arrived asking for information about a shipment of potassium from Italy to a Spanish port then in the hands of the Fascists. My secretary called her father.

"Let's go for a little drive," he said to me two days later, when he arrived in my office. "I want you to meet someone."

We stopped in a café outside of Paris, and there he introduced me to a somber but elegantly dressed American, who seemed to be in his late thirties and who spoke French with a strong accent.

"I hear you want to know about some potassium," he inquired mildly.

"Yes," I replied.

"Well, I think I just might have some information for you about the boat."

He did indeed give me very precise information about both cargo and itinerary, which I immediately telephoned to Negrín. Several years later, I met the man again at a cocktail party at the Museum of Modern Art in New York. We looked at each other across the room, but never exchanged a word. Later still, after the Second World War, I saw him at La Coupole with his wife. This time, we had a chat, during which he told me that he used to run a factory in the outskirts of Paris and had supported the Republican cause in various ways, which is how my secretary's father knew him.

During this time I was living in the suburb of Meudon. When I got home at night, I'd always stop, one hand on my gun, and check to make sure I hadn't been followed. We lived in a climate of fear and secrets and unknown forces, and as we continued to receive hourly bulletins on the progress of the war, we watched our hopes slowly dwindle and die.

It's not surprising that Republicans like myself didn't oppose the Nazi-Soviet pact. We'd been so disappointed by the Western democracies, who still treated the Soviet Union with contempt and refused all meaningful contact with its leaders, that we saw Stalin's gesture as a way of gaining time, of strengthening our forces, which, no matter what happened in Spain, were sure to be thrown into World War II. Most of the French Communist party also approved of the pact; Aragon made that clear more than once. One of the rare voices raised in protest within the party was that of the brilliant Marxist intellectual Paul Nizan. Yet we all knew that the pact wouldn't last, that, like everything else, it too would fall apart.

I remained sympathetic to the Communist party until the end of the 1950s, when I finally had to confront my revulsion. Fanaticism of any kind has always repelled me, and Marxism was no exception; it was like any other religion that claims to have found *the* truth. In the 1930s, for instance, Marxist doctrine permitted no mention of the unconscious mind or of the numerous and profound psychological forces in the individual. Everything could be explained, they said, by socioeconomic mechanisms, a notion that seemed perfectly derisory to me. A doctrine like that leaves out at least half of the human being.

I know I'm digressing; but, as with all Spanish picaresques, digression seems to be my natural way of telling a story. Now that I'm old and my memory is weaker, I have to be very careful, but I can't seem to resist beginning a story, then abandoning it suddenly for a seductive parenthesis, and by the time I finish, I've forgotten where I began. I'm always asking my friends: "Why am I telling you this?" And now I'm afraid I'll have to give in to one last digression.

There were all kinds of missions I had to carry out, one being that of Negrín's bodyguard from time to time. Armed to the teeth and backed up by the Socialist painter Quintanilla, I used to watch over Negrín at the Gare d'Orsay without his being aware of it. I also often slipped across the border into Spain, carrying "special" documents. It was on one of those occasions that I took a plane for the first time in my life, along with Juanito Negrín, the prime minister's son. We'd just flown over the Pyrenees when we saw a Fascist fighter plane heading toward us from the direction of Majorca. We were terrified, until it veered off suddenly and turned around, dissuaded perhaps by the DC-8 from Barcelona.

During a trip to Valencia, I went to see the head of agitprop to show him some papers that had come to us in Paris and which we thought might be useful to him. The following morning, he picked me up and drove me to a villa a few kilometers outside the city, where he introduced me to a Russian, who examined my documents and claimed to recognize them. Like the Falangists and the Germans, the Republicans and the Russians had dozens of contacts like this—the secret services were doing their apprenticeships everywhere. When a Republican brigade found itself besieged from the other side of the Gavarnie, French sympathizers smuggled arms to them across the mountains. In fact, throughout the war, smugglers in the Pyrenees transported both men and propaganda. In the area of St.-Jean-de-Luz, a brigadier in the French gendarmerie gave the smugglers no trouble if they were crossing the border with Republican tracts. I wish there'd been a more official way to show my gratitude, but I did give him a superb sword I'd bought near the place de la République, on which I'd had engraved: "For Services Rendered to the Spanish Republic."

Our relationship with the Fascists was exceedingly complex, as the García incident illustrates so well. García was an out-and-out crook who claimed to be a Socialist. During the early months of the war, he set up his racket in Madrid under the sinister name of the Brigada del Amanecer—the Sunrise Brigade. Early in the morning, he'd break into the houses of the well-to-do, "take the men for a walk," rape the women, and steal whatever he and his band could get their hands on. I was in Paris when a French union man who was working in a hotel came to tell me that a Spaniard was getting ready to take a ship for South America and that he was carrying a suitcase full of stolen jewels. It seemed that García had made his fortune, left Spain, and was skipping the continent altogether under an assumed name.

García was a terrible embarrassment to the Republic, but the Fascists were also desperate to catch him. The boat was scheduled for a stopover at Santa Cruz de Tenerife, which at that time was occupied by Franco. I passed my information along to the ambassador, and without a moment's hesitation he relayed it to the Fascists via a neutral embassy. When García arrived in Santa Cruz, he was picked up and hanged.

One of the strangest stories to emerge from the war was the Calanda pact. When the agitation began, the civil guard was ordered to leave Calanda and concentrate at Saragossa. Before leaving, however, the officers gave the job of maintaining order in the town to a sort of council made up of leading citizens, whose first venture was to arrest several notorious activists, including a well-known anarchist, a few Socialist peasants, and the only Communist. When the anarchist forces from Barcelona reached the outskirts of town at the beginning of the war, these notable citizens decided to pay a visit to the prison.

"We've got a proposition for you," they told the prisoners. "We're at war, and heaven only knows who's going to win. We're all Calandians, so we'll let you out on the condition that, whatever happens, all of us promise not to engage in any acts of violence whatsoever."

The prisoners agreed, of course, and were immediately released; a few days later, when the anarchists entered Calanda, their first act was to execute eighty-two people. Among the victims were nine Dominicans, most of the leading citizens on the council, some doctors and landowners, and even a few poor people whose only crime was a reputation for piety.

The deal had been made in the hope of keeping Calanda free from the violence that was tearing the rest of the country apart, to make the town a kind of no man's land; but neutrality was a mirage. It was fatal to believe that anyone could escape time or history.

Another extraordinary event that occurred in Calanda, and probably in many other villages as well, began with the anarchist order to go to the main square, where the town crier blew his trumpet and announced: "From today on, it is decreed that there will be free love in Calanda." As you can imagine, the declaration was received with utter stupefaction, and the only consequence was that a few women were harassed in the streets. No one seemed to know what free love meant, and when the women refused to comply with the decree, the hecklers let them go on their way with no complaints. To jump from the perfect rigidity of Catholicism to something called free love was no easy feat; the entire town was in a state of total confusion. In order to restore order, in people's minds more than anywhere else, Mantecon, the governor of Aragón, made an extemporaneous speech one day from the balcony of our house in which he declared that free love was an absurdity and that we had other, more serious things to think about, like a civil war.

By the time Franco's troops neared Calanda, the Republican sympathizers in the town had long since fled. Those who stayed to greet the Falangists had nothing to worry about. Yet if I can believe a Lazarist father who came to see me in New York, about a hundred people in Calanda were executed, so fierce was the Fascists' desire to remove any possible Republican contamination.

My sister Conchita was arrested in Saragossa after Republican planes had bombed the city (in fact, a bomb fell on the roof of the basilica without exploding, which gave the church an unparalleled opportunity to talk about miracles), and my brother-in-law, an army officer, was accused of having been involved in the incident. Ironically, he was in a Republican jail at that very moment. Conchita was finally released, but not before a very close brush with execution.

(The Lazarist father who came to New York brought me the portrait Dali had painted of me during our years at the Residencia. After he told me what had happened in Calanda, he said to me earnestly, "Whatever you do, don't go back there!" I had no desire whatsoever to go back, and many years were to pass before I did in fact return.)

In 1936, the voices of the Spanish people were heard for the first time in their history; and, instinctively, the first thing they attacked was the Church, followed by the great landowners—their two ancient enemies. As they burned churches and convents and massacred priests, any doubts anyone may have had about hereditary enemies vanished completely.

I've always been impressed by the famous photograph of those ecclesiastical dignitaries standing in front of the Cathedral of Santiago de Compostela in full sacerdotal garb, their arms raised in the Fascist salute toward some officers standing nearby. God and Country are an unbeatable team; they break all records for oppression and bloodshed.

I've never been one of Franco's fanatical adversaries. As far as I'm concerned, he wasn't the Devil personified. I'm even ready to believe that he kept our exhausted country from being invaded by the Nazis. Yes, even in Franco's case there's room for some ambiguity. And in the cocoon of my timid nihilism, I tell myself that all the wealth and culture on the Falangist side ought to have limited the horror. Yet the worst excesses came from them; which is why, alone with my dry martini, I have my doubts about the benefits of money and culture.

Spanish-born filmmaker Luis Buñuel recorded this account of the Civil War in his autobiography My Last Sigh *in 1983.*

PABLO NERUDA

A Few Things Explained

You will ask: And where are the lilacs?
And the metaphysics muffled in poppies?
And the rain which so often has battered
its words till they spouted up
gullies and birds?

I'll tell you how matters stand with me.

I lived for a time in suburban
Madrid, with its bells
and its clocks and its trees.

The face of Castile
could be seen from that place, parched,
like an ocean of leather.

                    People spoke of my house
as "the house with the flowers"; it exploded
geraniums: such a beautiful

house, with the
dogs and the small fry.
                    Remember, Raul?
Remember it, Rafael?
                    Federico, under the ground
there, remember it?
Can you remember my house with the balconies where
June drowned the dazzle of flowers in your teeth?

                    Ah, brother, my brother!
All
the voices were generous, the salt of the market place,
convocations of shimmering bread,
the stalls of suburban Argüelles with its statue
as wan as an inkwell in the sheen of the hake:
oil swam in the spoons,
a wild pandemonium
of fingers and feet overflowing the streets,
meters and liters, all the avid
quintessence of living,
                    fish packed in the stands,
a contexture of roofs in the chill of the sun
where the arrowpoints faltered;
potatoes, inflamed and fastidious ivory,
tomatoes again and again to the sea.

Till one morning everything blazed:
one morning bonfires
sprang out of earth
and devoured all the living;
since then, only fire,
since then, the blood and the gunpowder,
ever since then.

Bandits in airplanes, Moors
and marauders with seal rings and duchesses,
black friars and brigands signed with the cross, coming
out of the clouds to a slaughter of innocents:
the blood of the children was seen in the streets,
flowing easily out, in the habit of children.

Jackals abhorred by the jackal!
Spittle of stones that the thirst of the thistle rejected,
vipers despised by the viper!

In sight of you now, I have seen
Spain uplifting its blood
in a torrent
of knives and defiance, to carry you under!
Turncoats
and generals:
see the death of my house,
look well at the havoc of Spain:
out of dead houses it is metal that blazes
in place of the flowers,
out of the ditches of Spain
it is Spain that emerges,
out of the murder of children, a gunsight with eyes,
out of your turpitude, bullets are born
that one day will strike for the mark
of your hearts.

Would you know why his poems
never mention the soil or the leaves,
the gigantic volcanoes of the country that bore him?

Come see the blood in the streets,
come see
the blood in the streets,
come see the blood
in the streets!

Pablo Neruda was Chilean consul to Madrid from 1933 to 1937. Because of his radical anti-Fascist sentiments, he was recalled and expelled from his post. These poems are from the Selected Poems, *translated by Ben Belitt.*

DOROTHY PARKER

Who Might Be Interested

After dinner, when they were all back in the living-room, Mrs. Pemberton came. The host admitted her to the little square hall from which the company could be seen, and aided her in inching from her shoulders the heavy lengths of mink that wrapped her. Freed, she stood in red velvet as thin and dark as claret. Down her bared chest pearls glowed, as if with their own sweet secrets, and she wore on one shoulder a full-blown rose of rubies with emerald leaves and little, mean thorns of diamonds. Perfume seemed to wave from her visibly, as heat shimmers away from steel on an August day.

"Don't look at me," she said. "I'm just practically thrown together. I absolutely tore over here—I was just heartsick I couldn't get away earlier. Well, when you said over the 'phone you were only having a few people who might be interested, I was so flattered I could hardly bear it. *Might* be interested, for heaven's sake! With *him* here. Oh, show me which one he is!"

She leaned towards the living-room. The host's hands were full of mink; with his head, he indicated the tall man sitting on a sofa.

"Oh is *that* all he looks like!" she said. "For heaven's sake."

"What did you expect?" the host asked. "A beret?"

"I don't know," she said. "I always sort of think people ought to be sunburned, anyway, when they come back from places. They ought to *look* as if they'd been somewhere, don't you think so? Oh, honestly, I can't wait to meet him!"

She did not. She ran into the living-room, with gay flips of the hand for those she knew and ingratiating smiles for those she had not yet met, straight to the tall man. The host caught up with her, and made introductions. So swiftly that no separate motion was visible, she had a chair drawn up six inches in front of the tall man's knees, and was in it, with her chin on her palm, looking at his eyes. The young woman in the blue knitted dress who had been sitting next to him on the sofa moved across the room and sat down on the arm of the hostess's chair.

"Well, here I am!" Mrs. Pemberton said. "I'm your greatest fan, you know that? I've got all your books, and I keep giving them away to my friends."

"And they keep giving them back?" he said.

"Crazy!" she said. "Honestly, I'm just sick about not getting here earlier. All I must have missed! And there's a million things I want to ask you. Now please go ahead and tell me all about it. Tell me every single thing about China."

"I'd love to," he said. "But you see, I've never been to China. I've—"

"You *haven't?*" she said. "Well, then, where *have* you been?"

"Spain you see," he said. "I've just come back from Spain."

For some seconds, she was inarticulate with laughter. All she could do was writhe and bubble and make pushing motions at him with her hand, as if bidding him go 'way.

"Wouldn't you know I'd get them mixed up!" she said. "Well, you really can't blame me, after all, can you? Both terrible places. Spain, for heaven's sake! Well, tell me about it, I can't imagine what it's like."

"That comes from reading newspapers," he said.

"How did you happen to get hectic about Spain?" she said. "What did you want to go all the way over and get into that messy thing for? A person like you!"

"Because I was a person like you," he said. "I couldn't imagine what it was like."

"Now tell me again," she said, "which is the good side and which is the terrible one in that war, anyway? I haven't got it straight yet."

"Well, it's only been going on two and a half years," he said.

"Naturally," she said, "I know what it's all about, and who's on what side, of course, and all that, but I just can't get the names straight. I'm forever getting the Insurgents mixed up with the Rebels. Well, go on and tell me about it, anyway. Go ahead and depress me. Wasn't it all terrible?"

"No," he said. "Only some things were terrible."

"Oh, come on, now," she said. "Listen. Come on. It must have been *all* terrible. How could it *help* but be? You don't have to try to not say anything disagreeable in front of me. You can tell me anything you want. Honestly you can. Anything you could say to me wouldn't matter a bit, because I'm really interested. So you see you don't have to be nice. Go ahead and tell me what the terrible things were you were talking about."

"Well—hunger," he said. "Starvation. And women and children, killed in the streets by bombs."

"Now that's one thing you really can't ask me to get hectic about," she said. "Of course it's terrible and all that, but if people will go and get themselves into a war, why, that's what they've got to expect, that's all. I forgot to tell you, I'm absolutely against war. I definitely do not believe in it. Can you honestly tell me that you, as a civilized person, in this day and age, really believe in war?"

"No," he said. "Nor in hurricanes, either."

"I think everybody should keep out of things," she said. "That's what I believe. And if you'll pardon me, I think it's absolutely ridiculous for you, a great writer, probably an intelligent person, to go barging off to a place like Spain with a war going on that's none of anybody's business, when you ought to be thankful you have a country of your own to stay in where at least people aren't getting killed every day."

"I'm sure you're glad of those oceans we've got on each side of us, aren't you?" he said.

"I most certainly am!" she said. "And they're going to *stay* there, too. I just can't understand why you—Oh. Oh, *I* see. You're going to write a book about it, aren't you?"

"No," he said. "I shouldn't think so."

"Then why *did* you go?" she said.

"Well, I told you why I went," he said. "And now I'm

back, I thought I could tell people what I'd seen, and maybe raise some money. It's a dirty job, but that's what I'm trying to do."

"What *for*, for God's sake?" she said.

"For food," he said. "You don't know what a starving child is like until you've seen one. Until you've seen them by the thousand. They don't cry. Only you see their eyes. While you're there and after you're back, you see their eyes. I want to get help for those children. That's all."

Mrs. Pemberton leaned even closer to the tall man.

"Oh," she said, "I think that's perfectly wonderful of you. To get help for those children! Those little, little children!"

"They're just regulation size children," he said. "Or at least they would be, if they had food. You don't know, you can't realize, how those people in Spain need food!"

"I didn't know," she said. "I didn't know until you told me. Your voice! Now I know. Now I realize. Oh, we've *got* to do something for them! We've *got* to do something for General Franco and those poor, starving people!"

"Well, I—" the tall man said, and stopped. "You see," he said, with care, "I wasn't quite talking about Franco's side, exactly. They've got quite a lot of food in Franco's territory. I was on the other side, you see. It was the other side I meant, more. It's the other side where the children are hungry, where the women are—"

But Mrs. Pemberton had become veined marble in red velvet. She was straight against her chair; her stiffened fingers gripped the knobs of its arms. Her head was flung back, and she looked at the tall man down her delicate nose, with its nostrils distended.

"Well, really," she said. "After all, you know, I didn't come here to listen to Communism and atheism."

"When did you hear them?" he said.

"I think I have heard quite enough," she said. She rose. "Good-night."

The tall man rose, also. "Good-night," he said, and smiled at her. "I'm very sorry. Well. I guess you won't give away any more of my books, will you?"

Mrs. Pemberton smiled back at him. Thin ice seemed to tinkle along the contracting muscles of her face as she did so.

"I shall see," she said with great distinctness, "what I can do to-morrow about those that I have on my shelves. Good-night, again. It's been a *great pleasure*, I'm sure."

The tall man bowed.

In puffs of perfume like smoke from cannon-fire, Mrs. Pemberton swept over to her host. She breathed heavily at him.

"Really!" said Mrs. Pemberton. "Well, really!"

The tall man made for the young woman in the blue knitted dress. He stopped at her side.

"Christ!" said the tall man.

Dorothy Parker wrote this piece as a response to being labeled a "humorous" writer. The story was never published until this year in Mother Jones *magazine.*

THEODORE DREISER

Barcelona in August

We felt war immediately as we crossed the border of
Spain in an old car, and sped towards Barcelona. A sense
of impending catastrophe difficult to define at first.
Spain is beautiful. The air, the colour, the little farms,
many unchanged in appearance, have great charm. But
everything is infected by fear. A flight of birds may
startle you as if it were an air raid. In all the little villages, the central squares or market-places are cut across
by deep trenches into which people may throw themselves at the sound of the siren announcing aeroplanes.
As we near Barcelona, shell-shattered homes and villages
grow more frequent. I saw one village cut literally in
half by a shell. One part standing and with people going
about their business. The other smashed, wiped out,
dead. Then several villages I saw were completely
shattered, annihilated. Little villages, without any possible military significance. In these, most of the people
were gone. But there were usually a few old ones, sitting in the ruins of their homes, cooking, even, between

broken walls. In a certain village I saw only one old woman, sitting in a dream of misery.

Barcelona is a beautiful city. It is one of the fine cities of the world. I wish I could describe its charm beside the sea. It has great modern buildings, great powerful docks. Many have been destroyed, but it is still a magnificent city.

But five miles of serpentine subways cut under the city. They have built them irregularly, with openings at all sorts of unexpected spots, with several entrances at all central places. They have built them like rabbits' burrows, so that if one entrance or exit is blocked, they can escape by another. The passages are very clever and very deep. There is room for benches, in some places. In others real shelters, with running water, lights, have been prepared. Some people spend half the day in these places, when an air raid has been announced. Big sirens have usually time to announce a raid five minutes before the bombs can drop. Sometimes they keep screeching off and on for a whole day. There have been several three-day raids, when planes kept coming over the city again and again, not always to drop bombs, but to terrorize.

The hotel at which I stayed was a big handsome structure, in the most luxurious European style. Its kitchen had been carried partly away by a bomb. But business went on as usual. In the dining-room, waiters served on silver platters—one bun and the black juice they call coffee. There is no meat, no sugar, no butter, no milk. They serve a sort of pap, made out of vegetable matter. It is nourishing, to some extent, and fried with sauce, vaguely resembles meat. The heavy furniture and hangings are still there. But there are no sheets on the beds. All available linen or fine cloth has been taken for bandages for the wounded. There is no soap. In the whole of Barcelona, you cannot buy a piece of soap. When I had been there a few days, I developed an itch on my neck and cheek. I could get no soap nor ointment. At the drugstore, I was given a sort of herb, which had no effect on my neck whatsoever. I was told that all ointments or antiseptics were needed for the wounded. And over a third of the inhabitants of Barcelona are suffering from the 'itch' without any way of treating it. (It was only two weeks after I got back to Paris that I got rid of mine!)

The clothes of the people show what they endure. The clothes of the middle-class people are now as miserable as those of the poor. Their shoes are worn out, broken open, tied with strings. They go about on foot. Since one of the big power plants was destroyed, there are no street lights and no street-cars. A few official cars are the only means of getting about. Most horses and donkeys have disappeared. In the morning, you see little groups of people setting out on foot with sacks. They go out to forage in the country around Barcelona. They come back in the evening with a few sticks of fire wood, a cabbage, or a few turnips, etc., or with nothing at all. There are 12 million Loyalists in territory which before held about two million. They are slowly starving.

Suffering has brought out a marvellous spirit in the people which is stronger than anything you can imagine. I spoke to Del Vayo and Negrin. Del Vayo is a stocky, honest man in civilian clothes. Negrín, too, wears civilian clothes. They impress you as intellectuals rather than politicians. They said they had, in certain black moments, considered giving in, to save the people more suffering. But they were convinced that the people themselves would not give in. They would rather get new leaders and go on. Del Vayo said they can go on fighting for a year, a year and a half.

Such spirit as there is in Spain seems to me—well—beautiful.

Of course Hitler and Mussolini are backing Franco, but not to the extent he had hoped. On the other hand, France and Russia have not been helping the Loyalists nearly as much as has been thought. When I first arrived in Paris to attend a conference called by Bonnet of France and Lord Cecil of England, against the bombing of Open Cities, I was greatly surprised to find that the conference was a sort of diplomatic manoeuvre to reconcile other nations to England's attitude of Hands-off—the making of humanitarian phrases without humanitarian aims. In some measure, this prepared me for the attitude of Chamberlain and Daladier in the Czechoslovakian crisis. This indifference of certain powerful individuals representing England and France, to the fate of the Spanish Government. A protest was voiced against Hitler's treatment of Catholics, but no protest against Franco or Mussolini's bombing of Open Cities was allowed. The *Apasionara,* famous Loyalist woman envoy, was not allowed to speak. When they learned of my views on Spain at a luncheon just before I was to speak, they did everything to put my speech off, and only at the end of the session, as I still sat on the platform, were they obliged to call on me. (This speech was printed in *Direction* last month.) The next day I spoke at a French Writers' Congress which showed the true spirit of the French people towards Spain. But this spirit of sympathy and would-be co-operation, is everywhere blocked by those in authority. The Loyalists have large sums in the banks of Paris, which belong to the Government of Spain. But since Franco also claims these funds, financial powers have been able to keep them tied up 'till the end of the war'. The Loyalists need them desperately now, but are not even allowed credit against them. When I left Barcelona, I told Del Vayo I would telephone the French minister Bonnet to ask if he could send a few automobiles, urgently needed for transportation across the border. In Paris, Bonnet said he would see what could be done. But nothing was done, at least during the remaining two weeks of my stay in Europe.

Theodore Dreiser filed this report from Barcelona for Direction *in November 1938.*

SALVADOR DALI

Premonition of the Spanish Civil War

I was definitely not a historic man. On the contrary I felt myself essentially anti-historic and a-political. Either I was too much ahead of my time or much too far behind, but never contemporaneous with ping-pong-playing men. The disagreeable memory of having seen two Spaniards capable of indulging in that imbecile game filled me with shame. It was a dreadful omen: the ping-pong ball appeared to me as a little death's-head—empty, without weight, and catastrophic in its frivolity—the real death's-head, personifying politics completely skinned. And in the menacing silence that surrounded the tock, tock, tock, tock of the light skull of the ping-pong ball bouncing back and forth across the table I sensed the approach of the great armed cannibalism of our history, that of our coming Civil War, and the mere memory of the sound of the ping-pong ball heard on the historic night of October 6th was enough to set my teeth on edge in anticipation.

When I arrived in Paris I painted a large picture

which I entitled *Premonition of Civil War*. In this picture I showed a vast human body breaking out into monstrous excrescences of arms and legs tearing at one another in a delirium of autostrangulation. As a background to this architecture of frenzied flesh devoured by a narcissistic and biological cataclysm, I painted a geological landscape, that had been uselessly revolutionized for thousands of years, congealed in its "normal course." The soft structure of that great mass of flesh in civil war I embellished with a few boiled beans, for one could not imagine swallowing all that unconscious meat without the presence (however uninspiring) of some mealy and melancholy vegetable.

The first news of the Spanish Civil War that I had prophesied in my painting were not long in coming. I learned it in London, at a supper at the Savoy, after attending a concert of chamber music. I had asked for a poached egg, and this immediately brought up in my mind that ping-pong ball which had, in fact, been haunting me intermittently. It had, so to speak, just had time to mature. I communicated to the composer Igor Markevitch my idea of the lamentable and highly demoralizing effect that playing a game of ping-pong with a poached egg could produce—it would be almost worse than playing tennis with a dead bird. This poached egg set my teeth on edge, for I discovered, incomprehensibly, that it contained sand. I am sure that it was not the fault of the chef of the Savoy, but that it was the African sand of the history of Spain which had just risen to my mouth. Against sand, champagne! But I did not drink any. A period of ascetic rigor and of a quintessential violence of style was going to dominate my thinking and my tormented life, illuminated solely by the fires of faith of the Spanish Civil War and the esthetic fires of the

Renaissance—in which intelligence was one day to be reborn.

The Civil War had broken out! I knew it, I was sure of it, I had foreseen it! And Spain, spared by the other war, was to be the first country in which all the ideological and insoluble dramas of Post-War Europe, all the moral and esthetic anxiety of the "isms" polarized in those two words "revolution" and "tradition," were now to be solved in the crude reality of violence and of blood. The Spanish anarchists took to the streets of total subversion with black banners, on which were inscribed the words, VIVA LA MUERTE! (Long live death!). The others, with the flag of tradition, red and gold, of immemorial Spain bearing that other inscription which needed only two letters, FE (faith). And all at once, in the middle of the cadaverous body of Spain half devoured by the vermin and the worms of exotic and materialistic ideologies, one saw the enormous Iberian erection, like an immense cathedral filled with the white dynamite of hatred. To bury and to unbury! To unbury and to bury! To bury in order to unbury anew! Therein lay the whole carnal desire of the civil war of that land of Spain, too long passive and unsated, too long patient in suffering others to play the humiliating game of the vile and anecdotic ping-pong of politics on the aristocratic nobility of its back. Land of Spain, you who had been capable of fecundating religion itself! And this was what we were now to witness—what the land of Spain was capable of—a planetary capacity for suffering and inflicting suffering, for burying and unburying, for killing and resuscitating. For it was going to be necessary for the jackal claws of the revolution to scratch down to the atavistic layers of tradition in order that, as they became savagely ground and mutilated against the granitic hardness of the bones of this tradition they were profaning, one might in the end be dazzled anew by that hard light of the treasures of "ardent death" and of putrefying and resurrected splendors that this earth of Spain held hidden in the depths of its entrails. The past was unearthed, lifted to its feet, and the past walked among the living-dead, was armed—the flesh was resuscitated in the disinterment of the lovers of Teruel, people learned to love one another in killing one another. For nothing is closer to an embrace than a death-grapple. The militiaman of Faith would come to the café carrying on his arm the mummy of a twelfth-century nun whom he had just unearthed; he would not leave her! He wanted to bring her with him, fastened to his *correajes* as his "mascot," to the trenches on the Aragon front and die with her if need be. An old friend of the architect Gaudi claims to have seen the unearthed body of that architect of genius dragged through the streets of Barcelona by a rope that the children had fastened around his neck. He told me that Gaudi had been very well embalmed, and that he looked "exactly" as he had in the life, except that he did not look very well. This was after all only natural, considering the fact that Gaudi had been buried for some twenty years. In Vic the soldiers played football every afternoon with the head of the archbishop of Vic, in Vic . . .

From all parts of martyred Spain rose a smell of incense, of chasubles, of burned curates' fat and of quartered spiritual flesh, which mingled with the smell of hair dripping with the sweat of promiscuity from that other flesh, concupiscent and as paroxysmally quartered, of the mobs fornicating among themselves and with death. And all this rose toward heaven like the very odor of ecstasy of the orgasm of revolution.

The anarchists lived their dream in which they had never wholly believed. Now they did in fact enter the office of the notary public and perform their intimate functions right on his desk, which stood as the symbol of property. In several villages in which integral libertarianism was set up, all the bank notes were burned.

The Spanish Civil War changed none of my ideas. On the contrary it endowed their evolution with a decisive rigor. Horror and aversion for every kind of revolution assumed in me an almost pathological form. Nor did I want to be called a reactionary. This I was not: I did not "react"—which is an attribute of unthinking matter. For I simply continued to think, and I did not want to be called anything but Dali. But already the hyena of public opinion was slinking around me, demanding of me with the drooling menace of its expectant teeth that I make up my mind at last, that I become Stalinist or Hitlerite. No! No! No! and a thousand times no! I was going to continue to be as always and until I died, Dalinian and only Dalinian! I believed neither in the communist revolution nor in the national-socialist revolution, nor in any other kind of revolution. I believed only in the supreme reality of tradition.

Besides, revolutions have never interested me by what they "revolutionize," which is always perishable and constantly threatened with becoming the opposite of what it was at the beginning. If revolutions are interesting it is solely because in revolutionizing they disinter and recover fragments of the tradition that was believed dead because it had been forgotten, and that needed simply the spasm of revolutionary convulsions to make them emerge, so that they might live anew. And through the revolution of the Spanish Civil War there was going to be rediscovered nothing less than the authentic catholic tradition peculiar to Spain, that wholly categorical and fanatical catholicism, that passion built of stone, massive with granitic and calcareous reality which is Spain.* In the Spanish Civil War the Spanish people, the aristocracy of peoples, even while they were devouring one another, were obscurely and unknowingly fighting unanimously for one thing, for that thing which is Spain—ardent tradition. All—atheists, believers, saints, criminals, grave-openers and grave-diggers, executioners and martyrs—all fought with the unique courage and pride of the crusaders of faith. For all were Spaniards, and even the most ferocious sacrileges and manifestations of atheism abounded in faith, illuminating the dark dementia of unleashed and omnipotent passion with flashes of heaven.

The story has often been told of the Andalusian anarchist who during the Civil War walked up the steps of a gutted and profaned church with the grace of a torero, drew himself up to his full height before a crucifix whose Christ wore long natural hair, and after having insulted Him with the most atrocious blasphemies, spat into His face while with one hand he brutally seized the long hair which he was about to tear out. At this moment the Christ's hand became detached from the cross and His arm, which was articulated, fell on the shoulder of the Andalusian soldier, who dropped dead on the spot. What a believer! . . .

At the very outbreak of the revolution my great friend, the poet of *la mala muerte*, Federico García

---

* "Spain is a granitic or calcareous plateau with a mean altitude of 700 metres." *(Petit Larousse.)*

Lorca, died before a firing squad in Granada, occupied by the fascists. His death was exploited for propaganda purposes. This was ignoble, for they knew as well as I that Lorca was by essence the most a-political person on earth. Lorca did not die as a symbol of one or another political ideology, he died as the propitiatory victim of that total and integral phenomenon that was the revolutionary confusion in which the Civil War unfolded. For that matter, in the civil war people killed one another not even for ideas, but for "personal reasons," for reasons of personality; and like myself, Lorca had personality and to spare, and with it a better right than most Spaniards to be shot by Spaniards. Lorca's tragic sense of life was marked by the same tragic constant as that of the destiny of the whole Spanish people.

Lorca's death, and the repercussions of the civil war which had begun to create a suffocating atmosphere of partisanship in the heart of Paris, made me decide to leave this city to go and dedicate the whole energy of my thinking to my work of esthetic cosmogony and synthesis which Gala had "inspired" in me at the time of my mortal anguish in Port Lligat. I set off on a voyage through Italy.

The disasters of war and revolution in which my country was plunged only intensified the wholly initial violence of my esthetic passion, and while my country was interrogating death and destruction, I was interrogating that other sphinx, of the imminent European "becoming," that of the RENAISSANCE. I knew that after Spain, all Europe would sink into war as a consequence of the communist and fascist revolutions, and from the poverty and collapse of collectivist doctrines would arise a medieval period of reactualization of individual, spiritual and religious values. Of these imminent Middle Ages I wanted to be the first, with a full understanding of the laws of the life and death of esthetics, to be able to utter the word "renaissance."

This excerpt from The Secret Life of Salvador Dali *was published in 1942. Translated by Haakon M. Chevalier.*

W. H. AUDEN

Spain

Yesterday all the past. The language of size
Spreading to China along the trade-routes; the diffusion
    Of the counting-frame and the cromlech;
Yesterday the shadow-reckoning in the sunny climates.

Yesterday the assessment of insurance by cards,
The divination of water; yesterday the invention
    Of cartwheels and clocks, the taming of
Horses. Yesterday the bustling world of the navigators.

Yesterday the abolition of fairies and giants,
The fortress like a motionless eagle eyeing the valley,
    The chapel built in the forest;
Yesterday the carving of angels and alarming gargoyles;

The trial of heretics among the columns of stone;
Yesterday the theological feuds in the taverns
    And the miraculous cure at the fountain;
Yesterday the Sabbath of witches; but to-day the struggle.

Yesterday the installation of dynamos and turbines,
The construction of railways in the colonial desert;
    Yesterday the classic lecture
On the origin of Mankind. But to-day the struggle.

Yesterday the belief in the absolute value of Greek,
The fall of the curtain upon the death of a hero;
    Yesterday the prayer to the sunset
And the adoration of madmen. But to-day the struggle.

As the poet whispers, startled among the pines,
Or where the loose waterfall sings compact, or upright
    On the crag by the leaning tower:
"O my vision. O send me the luck of the sailor."

And the investigator peers through his instruments
At the inhuman provinces, the virile bacillus
    Or enormous Jupiter finished:
"But the lives of my friends. I inquire. I inquire."

And the poor in their fireless lodgings, dropping the
    sheets
Of the evening paper: "Our day is our loss, O show us
    History the operator, the
Organiser, Time the refreshing river."

And the nations combine each cry, invoking the life
That shapes the individual belly and orders
    The private nocturnal terror:
"Did you not found the city state of the sponge,

"Raise the vast military empires of the shark
And the tiger, establish the robin's plucky canton?
    Intervene. O descend as a dove or
A furious papa or a mild engineer, but descend."

And the life, if it answers at all, replies from the heart
And the eyes and the lungs, from the
                              shops and squares of the city:
    "O no, I am not the mover;
Not to-day; not to you. To you, I'm the

"Yes-man, the bar-companion, the easilyduped;
I am whatever you do. I am your vow to be
    Good, your humorous story.
I am your business voice. I am your marriage.

"What's your proposal? To build the just city? I will.
I agree. Or is it the suicide pact, the romantic
    Death? Very well, I accept, for
I am your choice, your decision. Yes, I am Spain."

Many have heard it on remote peninsulas,
On sleepy plains, in the aberrant fishermen's islands
    Or the corrupt heart of the city,
Have heard and migrated like gulls or the seeds of a
    flower.

They clung like burrs to the long expresses that lurch
Through the unjust lands, through the night,
                              through the alpine tunnel;
    They floated over the oceans;
They walked the passes. All presented their lives.

On that arid square, that fragment nipped off from hot
Africa, soldered so crudely to inventive Europe;
    On the tableland scored by rivers,
Our thoughts have bodies; the menacing shapes of our
    fever

Are precise and alive. For the fears which made us
   respond
To the medicine ad. and the brochure of winter cruises
     Have become invading battalions;
And our faces, the institute-face, the chain-store, the ruin

Are projecting their greed as the firing squad and the
   bomb.
Madrid is the heart. Our moments of tenderness blossom
     As the ambulance and the sandbag;
Our hours of friendship into a people's army.

To-morrow, perhaps the future. The research on fatigue
And the movements of packers; the gradual exploring
   of all the
     Octaves of radiation;
To-morrow the enlarging of consciousness by diet and
                  breathing.

To-morrow the rediscovery of romantic love,
The photographing of ravens; all the fun under
     Liberty's masterful shadow;
To-morrow the hour of the pageant-master and the
   musician,

The beautiful roar of the chorus under the dome;
To-morrow the exchanging of tips on the breeding of
   terriers,
     The eager election of chairmen
By the sudden forest of hands. But to-day the struggle.

To-morrow for the young the poets exploding like
   bombs,

The walks by the lake, the weeks of perfect communion;
    To-morrow the bicycle races
Through the suburbs on summer evenings. But to-day
                       the struggle.

To-day the deliberate increase in the chances of death,
The conscious acceptance of guilt in the necessary
    murder;
        To-day the expending of powers
On the flat ephemeral pamphlet and the boring meeting.

To-day the makeshift consolations: the shared cigarette,
The cards in the candlelit barn, and the scraping concert,
    The masculine jokes; to-day the
Fumbled and unsatisfactory embrace before hurting.

The stars are dead. The animals will not look.
We are left alone with our day, and the time is short, and
    History to the defeated
May say Alas but cannot help nor pardon.

See page 19 for a note on Auden and this poem.

ANDRÉ MALRAUX

The Peasants

As soon as the requisition order for the Italian lorries
came in from headquarters, Manuel had left Ximenes.
He walked back to the place where his Brigade was quartered, with the wolfhound trotting composedly beside
him, while Gartner busied himself returning the lorries
that had been scrounged before the battle.

The soldiers were wandering about Brihuega, empty-
handed and unwontedly at a loose end. The main street
with its pink and yellow houses, austere churches and
huge convents, was so full of rubbish, so many shattered
houses had disgorged their furniture into the roadway,
and the whole street was so closely linked up with the
war that, now there was a cessation of hostilities, it
seemed unreal, preposterous as the tombs and temples
of an extinct race, and the soldiers roaming it now without their rifles had the lost look of civilian unemployed.

Some streets, however, seemed unscathed by war.
Garcia had told Manuel how at Jaipur in India all the

house-fronts are painted in sham perspective and how each house wears in front of it, like a mask, its pink façade. Many of the Brihuega streets brought to mind a city not of mud but of the dead; death was lurking behind the windows that stood half open on the cheerless sky and the gay house-fronts that recalled siesta and the holiday season.

It seemed to Manuel that he heard the plash of fountains everywhere. A thaw had set in. Water was gushing from the stone corbels and along the gutters, fraying into little rivulets between the pointed cobble-stones so typical of old Spain and tumbling over them with the sound of miniature mountain-torrents, amid the pictures, scraps of furniture, pots and pans, and miscellaneous wreckage in the street. Not an animal had stayed in Brihuega; but now, like homeless cats, the *milicianos* were to be seen prowling from one street to another, in the desolation murmurous with running water.

As Manuel approached the centre of the town another sound mingled with the plash of water, in a counterpoint of limpid harmonies—the notes of a piano. The front wall of a house he was passing had collapsed into the street, leaving all the dwelling-rooms open to the sky; in one of them a *miliciano* was picking out the notes of a popular song with one finger. Manuel listened attentively; now across the water-music of the street he could make out the sounds of three pianos. Nothing like the *International*. The tunes were those of sentimental refrains, but played so slowly that they might have been in homage to the infinite pathos of the slopes, strewn with derelict lorries, that rose from Brihuega towards the livid sky.

Manuel had told Gartner that he had given up music, but he suddenly realized that what he needed most at this moment—alone in the street of a conquered town —was to hear some music. He had no desire to play, himself, and he wanted to remain alone. There were two gramophones in the Brigade mess-room. He had discarded the records which he had carried about with him in the early days of the war, but the big gramophone cabinet was well stocked. Gartner was a German.

He found some Beethoven symphonies and the *Adieux*. He was no more than a half-hearted admirer of Beethoven, but that made no difference. Taking the smaller gramophone into his room, he set it going. Now that the tension of his will relaxed, the past came into its own. He remembered his exact gesture when he had handed his revolver to Alba. Perhaps, as Ximenes said, he had found the life he was meant for. He was born to war, born to the responsibility of death. Like the sleep-walker who wakes up suddenly on the edge of a roof, he felt the dying cadence of the music bringing home to him the terrible precariousness of his mental foothold; any false step might land him in—a shambles! Another memory crossed his mind—of a blind beggar he had seen in Madrid on the night of Carabanchel. Manuel had been with the Chief of Police, in his car, when suddenly the headlights had lit up a blind man's outstretched fingers, magnifying their form, against the steep upward slope of the Gran Via, to a prodigious size, showing them humped and gnarled against the cobbles, criss-crossed by the pavements, and momentarily effaced by the few cars which the war had not driven from the streets—long, groping hands, long as the hands of Fate.

"Kilometre 95! Kilometre 95!" men were shouting in all parts of the town, always with the same intonation.

He felt the seething life around him charged with portents, as though some blind destiny lay in wait for him behind those lowering cloudbanks which the guns no longer racked. The wolfhound was listening, lying full length like the dogs in bas-reliefs. Some day there would be peace. And he, Manuel, would become another man, someone he could not visualize as yet; just as the soldier he had become could no more visualize the Manuel who once had bought a little car to go skiing in the Sierra.

Most likely it was the same with all those others moving through the streets, and the same with the men he could hear strumming their favourite tunes on pianos open to the public gaze—the men whose heavy pointed cowls had led the battle yesterday. Once it had been deliberate contemplation that had taught Manuel about himself; now it fell to chance to snatch him from the activities of the moment and force his mind upon his past. And, like himself, like all those others, drained of her blood, Spain, too, was growing conscious of herself —as in the hour of death, suddenly, a man takes stock of all his life. . . . But war may be discovered only once in a lifetime; life, many times.

As the strands of melody took form, interwoven with his past, they conveyed to him the selfsame message that the dim sky, those ageless fields and that town which had stopped the Moors might, too, have given him. For the first time Manuel was hearing the voice of that which is more awe-inspiring even than the blood of men, more enigmatic even than their presence on the earth—the infinite possibilities of their destiny. And he felt that this new consciousness within him was linked up with the sounds of running water in the street and the footfalls of the prisoners, profound and permanent as the beating of his heart.

André Malraux organized and commanded the international Republican Air Force, and toured the United States and Europe raising money for the Loyalists. He wrote what is generally considered the literary masterpiece of the war, Man's Hope *(1938). "The Peasants" is an excerpt from* Man's Hope.

EDNA ST. VINCENT MILLAY

Say That We Saw Spain Die

Say that we saw Spain die. O splendid bull, how well
    you fought!
Lost from the first.
. . . the tossed, the replaced, the watchful torero with
    gesture elegant and spry,
Before the dark, the tiring but the unglazed eye
    deploying the bright cape,
Which hid for once not air, but the enemy indeed,
    the authentic shape,
A thousand of him, interminably into the ring released
    . . . the turning beast at length between converging
    colors caught.

Save for the weapons of its skull, a bull
Unarmed, considering, weighing, charging
Almost a world, itself without ally.

Say that we saw the shoulders more than the mind
    confused, so profusely

Bleeding from so many more than the accustomed
    barbs, the game gone vulgar, the rules abused.

Say that we saw Spain die from loss of blood, a rustic
    reason, in a reinforced
And proud punctilious land, no *espada*—
A hundred men unhorsed,
A hundred horses gored, and the afternoon aging,
    and the crowd growing restless (all, all so much
    later than planned),
And the big head heavy, sliding forward in the sand,
    and the tongue dry with sand—no *espada*
Toward that hot neck, for the delicate and final thrust,
    having dared trust forth his hand.

Edna St. Vincent Millay's "Say That We Saw Spain Die"
originally appeared in Harpers *magazine, October 1938.*

John Miller has worked at *Esquire* and *Vanity Fair*. He is currently the publisher and editor of *Equator*, a new West Coast arts and literature magazine.